Creation, Chaos and Christ

Keswick 2008

Edited by Ali Hull

Authentic

MILTON KEYNES • COLORADO SPRINGS • HYDERABAD

Keswick
ministries
bringing the Word alive

First published 2008 by Authentic Media
9 Holdom Avenue, Bletchley, Milton Keynes, MK1 1QR, UK
1820 Jet Stream Drive, Colorado Springs, CO 80921, USA
Media, Medchal Road, Jeedimetla Village, Secunderabad 500 055, A.P., India
www.authenticmedia.co.uk
Authentic Media is a division of IBS-STL U.K., limited by guarantee, with its
Registered Office at Kingstown Broadway, Carlisle, Cumbria CA3 0HA.
Registered in England & Wales No. 1216232. Registered charity 270162

The right of Ali Hull to be identified as the Editor of this work has been
asserted by her in accordance with Copyright, Designs and Patents Act 1988

British Library Cataloguing in Publication Data

A catalogue record for this book is available from
the British Library
ISBN 978-1-85078-836-2

Cover design by fourninezero design.
Photography © Nigel Cooke, Neil Edbrooke and Kath Williams
Print Management by Adare
Printed in Great Britain by J.H. Haynes & Co., Sparkford

Contents

The Bible Readings

The Lectures and Seminars

The Addresses

Introduction by the Chairman of the 2008 Convention

The overwhelming response of Conventioners to the teaching this year was 'You dealt with relevant subjects in an extremely helpful way.' I heard this regularly during the Convention and letters received since have confirmed this view. This is a great encouragement to those of us who have responsibility for this event... Our desire is to so teach the word of God that Christ will be glorified and his people enabled to live for him in what seems to be an ever more challenging context.

For those of you who attended the Convention, I trust that what follows will be a reminder of the way God spoke to us through his servants during those days together. If you are reading this and were not at Keswick this year, have not been for many years, or may never have been, I pray that this will act as an encouragement to attend. Keswick is a special place: the magnificence of God's creation, combined with the opportunity to hear the word, ministered by those gifted by God to do so, leads so often to people having fresh dealings with the living God. That of course is the reason we convene. The purpose is not merely to increase our knowledge of the content of the Bible, but to meet with God, whom the Bible reveals to us.

I am typing out this Foreword in the evening after spending most of the day planning next year's Convention. I hope you will be with us.

Peter Maiden

Editor's Introduction

Each year we face the same set of questions regarding the contents of the Keswick Year book, which aims, amongst other things, to give as wide an impression of the event as we can, while still maintaining an emphasis on the biblical exposition which characterise the Convention. So this year along with the evening teaching, the seminars and the Bible readings, we have decided to add one other element – a piece of drama written and performed by Richard Hasnip of Saltmine Theatre. It is placed straight after Liam Goligher's teaching and complements it beautifully.

We were also faced with the question of what do we do with the Bible readings? Lately, we have turned some Bible reading series into separate study guides, but it was felt this year that would not be feasible, and so for the first time we have selected three of each set of five Bible readings – so you will find some, but not all, of the teaching of David Cook, Liam Goligher and Charles Price. For those looking for the John Lennox lecture, this, we hope, will come out separately at a later date. We have, however, included both the other two lectures, one on ecology from Christopher Wright and one on bioethics, by Dr John Wyatt. Altogether, we have aimed for a balance of teaching material. I hope those who were at the event and those who were not but would have liked to have been will all enjoy this volume as much as I have enjoyed working on it.

Ali Hull
Bristol, September 2008

The Bible Readings

Seeing the world God's way: Genesis 1 – 4

by David Cook

David Cook

David Cook is Principal of Sydney Missionary and Bible College and Director of the SMBC School of Preaching. He is a graduate of SBMC and Moore College, and has served as a Presbyterian minister in both rural New South Wales and the inner western suburbs of Sydney. David has been Principal of SMBC since 1986, lectures in preaching and pastoral subjects, and speaks at Christian conferences in Australia and overseas. Married to Maxine, they have five adult children, of whom four are married, and eight grandchildren. His interests include family, cricket, rugby (union and league) and coffee.

1 Elohim is awesome: Genesis 1:1 – 2:3

Introduction

Beginnings are of vital importance. They set the scene, they create an atmosphere, they establish a platform. So how does the Book of books begin? In Genesis 1:1 you have the executive summary: 'In the beginning God created the heavens and the earth.' There are seven words in Hebrew, translated into ten words in English. When Calvin began his great tome *The Institutes of the Christian Religion*, he said that true wisdom consists of two parts: knowledge of God and of ourselves. If you're looking for a true knowledge of God and a true knowledge of yourself, that is what the Bible is all about.

Look at verse 1: 'In the beginning, Elohim . . .' His name is in the plural, but it takes the singular verb to stress his majesty and his intensity. He 'created': he brought something out of nothing. The writer of the Hebrew says that what can be seen came out of that which was invisible. Elohim is the subject of the verb 'create', he is never the object, no one created Elohim, he is the great uncreated Creator. Verse 1 introduces us to our main themes: there's rest and creation here, but the focus of our attention is God: 'In the beginning, Elohim'. He made this awesome creation: how awesome is he?

Where we go to church in Sydney we're close to one of the large universities, and often post-doctoral students come from overseas.

Recently a man with a great scientific background joined our congregation from the United States, and his name was Rob. We got talking one day and I said, 'Rob, if I took a five cent piece and I put that piece in the middle of the Australian continent, would that five cent piece represent our solar system, with the Australian continent as the universe?' He said, 'No. Our solar system is a grain of sand. We have one sun in our solar system. But there are a billion suns in our galaxy, and in the universe there are about four billion galaxies.' How awesome is the universe in which we live? I said, 'How does our solar system compare to the size of the universe?' He said, 'It would be one to ten with thirty-seven zeros.' Elohim is awesome.

This morning I want to say seven things to you . . .

Elohim is powerful

. . . and the first is this: Elohim is powerful. He is the reality behind the creation: one sovereign, powerful, purposeful God. Look at Genesis 1:3; 'God said, "Let there be light," and [with a word] there was light.' Verse 5: 'God called the light "day" and the darkness he called "night."' Here in this chapter we see that God's word, his speech, is used fourteen times. It is effective. Seven times we are told 'It was so' and that which he called into being was good. The seventh time when he says that is in verse 31; 'God saw all that he had made, and it was very good.' To the Hebrew mind the number seven or a multiple of seven is special. It is the number of perfection, of wholeness, of fullness: it indicates Elohim's presence.

Elohim is methodical

He creates out of chaos, and the reporting of that creation is rhythmically beautiful. Look at day one, (v3): he creates the light. Day two (v6): he creates the sky and the sea. Day three, the double act of creation (vs 9–11): he creates the land and the plants. Day four (v14) parallels day one, the light: now he creates the sun, the moon and the stars. Day five (v20) parallels day two: in day two you have the sky and the sea, now you have the birds for the sky and the fish for the sea. Then day six (v24) paralleling with land and plants: God makes the land animals and man. It is beautifully methodical and well organised. It is this organised order that makes scientific experimentation and observation possible.

Look at the contrast to this. Go back to verse 2: what did God begin with? Chaos. But Elohim was active. His name occurs here thirty-five times: seven times five. Seven times he saw, seven times he said it was good, fourteen times he said or called things into being, there are seven days of creation, there are the seven words of verse 1. The number seven is like the Nike tick, it is the author's way of saying that Elohim is here, he is active, and creation is the product of his handiwork.

Elohim is the Protector and Benefactor of his creation

He is not aloof, he is not disinterested, he is involved. In this account, he names the day and the night. He names the expanse: 'I'll call it sky. The dry ground I'll call land; the gathered waters I will call sea.' He gives value to things: he says that's good, the sky is good; those seas, they're good; those plants, they're good; those stars, they're good; those creatures, they're good; that man, everything I have made, is very good. He says to man (and enables him); 'You fill the earth and subdue it, you rule it.' Elohim is the Blesser, the caring Provider, the Enabler, the Craftsman, the Benefactor, the Director. That's Elohim, our God.

Elohim creates a being who is like him (vs 22-30)

On the sixth day he creates man and, just so that we don't get too big a view of ourselves, we share the day with the land animals. We are both made out of dust, both commissioned to be fruitful and multiply, but the stress here is on the uniqueness of what God does now (v26): 'Let us make man.' Who is this 'us'? Is this an allusion to the Trinity? Probably not. Is it the royal we? Probably not. Elohim here is probably speaking to the angels in the heavenly court.

Look at verse 27 and the intensity: three times we are told God creates – 'God created man,' 'he created him,' 'he created them'. In the early pagan accounts man was an afterthought, created in order to feed the gods. Here man is the pinnacle, and you don't have a dependent god who needs to be fed, but dependent man who needs to be provided for by God. Three times we are told that we have been created in God's image: 'Let us make man in our image, in our likeness'. We are small but we are significant. I see, God sees; I hear, God hears. I speak, God speaks; I relate, God relates. I work, God works; I appreciate, God appreciates. I rule, God rules; I can be creative, God is creative. What drives us? We have a moral will: we are made in the image of God. I can be faithful, just as God is faithful, even when it is hard to be faithful. God makes responsible beings who are like him.

God's long-term strategy for creation is rest: Gen. 2:1–3

God didn't rest out of necessity. Three times we are told in verses 2-3, and it is stressed, 'by the seventh day . . . on the seventh day . . . the seventh day'. God blessed the seventh day, and each of these three verses is seven words in the Hebrew language. Notice that God did not cease creating on the sixth day. The way humankind lives today is that we think God stopped at day six. Everything that we can see here is vitally important to us: 'Let us live for the day, let us live for the six days, let's eat and drink, for tomorrow we die!' But God didn't stop at day six. 'I need to be productive in life;' that's stopping at day six. That is the fool. The fool lives for the six days, but God didn't stop at day six. All the other days have an evening and a morning, but this is a day which is to never end.

This seventh day is a day of endless rest, where God can sit back with his people and enjoy all that he has made. It is the eternal seventh day, every day is to be a seventh day. How foolish it is to live just for the six! God says 'Let's enjoy it in fellowship together. There is a seventh day!' By the book of Exodus, this day is one in a cycle of seven. The seventh day now becomes a glimpse into the way life was, the way life was meant to be, and a glimpse into the future. It anticipates the new creation. By the time we get to the New Testament, the Sabbath has become an instrument of oppression, and

Jesus has to say to the religious authorities, God didn't make the Sabbath for its own good, he made it for man's good. Man is not here to be fodder for the monster called the Sabbath.

When it comes to the Sabbath, all of the commandments are taken up in the New Testament apart from this one! Under the new covenant, the apostle Paul says the Sabbath is a shadow, but we now have the reality of rest, a relationship and righteousness in Christ. So he says don't let anyone judge you by a Sabbath-day, that's just a shadow of things to come. The reality of rest is found in Christ. The apostle Paul says let no one argue about the location of the day or the definition of the appropriate activity for the day. He says one man considers one day more sacred than another, another man considers every day alike. These are disputable matters. Don't argue about them.

I go to a gymnasium, run by a physiotherapist. There's only six to eight of us at any one time, and most of us are getting on in life. We always are debating some issue and consistently I feel I'm being left behind. We can be debating step one, and then step one is taken and we move on to step two and I want to go back to step one. Let me give you an example. They were debating whether or not it is possible to be a practising Christian and a practising homosexual – step one. They ticked that off, that's approved, let's go to step two: can this practising Christian who is a practising homosexual be ordained to Christian ministry? We're now into step two, but I want to go back to step one and argue whether it is appropriate to be a practising Christian and a practising homosexual.

It is exactly that way when it comes to scientific evolutions. Step one in the debate: modern science disproves the fact that there can be a God of Genesis who calls everything into being. Therefore step two: where did we come from? Did we evolve from some alien life form from the planet Mars? And I think, I want to go back to step one! What has modern science proven and disproved? Modern science can't prove God and it can't disprove God. Modern science doesn't have an experiment for God, modern science cannot then just write off God and say there is no God.

Modern science has a theory that things sprang into being by a random process, and they continue by the random process of natural selection; that things evolve from a simple to a complex life form. We are just gene machines. Let science have its theory, but science must be kept in its place. This is only a theory. Don't take the theory and turn it into a philosophy of life, because it is an empty philosophy of life.

I am not a random fatalist, I am not a materialist. Why? Because in the beginning, God created the heavens and the earth. That will not allow me to be a random fatalist, believing that life is full of random accidents. There is an intelligent, purposeful Creator. Genesis 1 won't allow me to be a materialist, thinking that I'm just a combination of cells, all I am is what you see.

Unless we keep science in its place we will have an escalating drug problem, where people look for the meaning for life in a bottle. We will have the despair of rising teenage suicide and knife attacks. What is life all about? It's meaningless, it's random, it's fatalistic! What's the point? We'll have the epidemic of depression. It's all the fruit of fatalistic, accidental, random materialism, and it will keep widening and deepening. I am not an atheist. I am not a polytheist, I do not believe there are many gods, I am not a pantheist. Everything in Genesis chapter 1 at some stage in the history of humankind has been worshipped. I am not a secularist: someone who says you can be most human when you are most apart from God. I believe that in the beginning, God created the heavens and the Earth, and in him all things hold together.

So what am I?

I've been a Christian long enough to know that there are so many Christians who all claim to believe, some more strongly than others, that they can give you a detailed account of how God created the universe. I don't want to offend anyone, and I don't want to enter into endless debates, but I do know that when real, regenerate, born-again Christians differ on an issue, the issue that they differ on cannot be vital. By believing one view or not believing another will not make me a Christian, nor will it disqualify me from being a Christian.

I had a young man come to me recently and say 'If I become a Christian, do I have to believe that God created the world in six twenty-four hour days? If I become a Christian, do I have to believe that Jonah was in the belly of a fish for three nights?' You could substitute 'If I become a Christian, do I have to believe some detail of Christ's return? Or some particular mode of baptism? Or some particular structure of Church government?' I said to this young man 'No. To become a Christian you only have to believe one thing, and when you come to that one, then we'll work on all those other things.'

To become a Christian you only need to believe one thing. The duplicate of Genesis 1 'In the beginning' is John 1. In the beginning, we are made in God's image. That image, as you know, is marred and damaged because of sin but, through Jesus, God restores and starts rebuilding that image. Just as there are seven days in creation, so John's gospel is marked by seven signs. On seven occasions, the Lord Jesus says 'I am'. He is showing himself, that he is the Lord of the new creation.

Verse 1 says: 'In the beginning was the Word, and the Word was with God, and the Word was God.' Look at verse 3: 'through him all things were made.' The apostle Paul says that all things were made through him and all things were made for the Word. He is the awesome Creator. Verse 4: 'In him was life, and that life was the light of men.' We come from the abstract Word, this philosophical concept, and the Word comes here, to this pinprick of a planet, in this tiny solar system. This Word came in the first century, to Palestine. This Word who was God and who was with God from all eternity has come here, into time and space. Verse 14, 'The Word became flesh and made his dwelling among us. We have seen his glory, the glory of the One and Only, who came from the Father, full of grace and truth.'

God so loved this tiny planet that he visited us. He so valued us that he came to restore us. We have been visited by our Creator, this little five-cent piece of a solar system, this little grain of sand called planet Earth. God has come here? What sort of a reception did we give him? Verse 10 says, 'He was in the world, and though the world was made through him, the world did not recognise him.' But what about if he came to his own, verse 11? 'He came to that which was his own, but his own did not receive him.' By contrast, verse 12 states, 'Yet to all who received him, those who believed in his name, he gave the right to become children of God'.

When John wrote those words under the inspiration of the Spirit, he sandwiches the great privilege of being a child of God between the conditions of that privilege: that is 'to all who received him, those who believed in his name' . . . to them 'he gave the right to become children of God.' We are all made in the image of God but those who received the Word and those who believed in his name uniquely have the privilege of calling the Creator their Father, of having their image restored and of becoming as mankind was intended to be.

Earlier this year I was in Vanuatu, ministering to Vanuatuan pastors. When John Paton, the first missionary, went to Vanuatu, he started by translating the gospel of John, and he kept coming on the word 'believe' and with his language helper, he could not find the equivalent in the New Vanuatuan language for the word 'believe'.

One day he was out with his language helper, trekking for a full day and at the end of the day they came back to their base camp and the language helper collapsed in his hammock. John Paton said 'What is the expression to describe you collapsing in exhaustion into your hammock?' It was that awkward expression which Paton used in the New Vanuatuan language to translate the word believe: to rest entirely, to collapse exhausted, into the Word who has become flesh and dwelt among us, full of grace and truth.

Recently I went to my dentist. He said 'You need root canal therapy. Here's a leaflet, take it home and read all about it.' I said 'I don't want your leaflet, I don't want to read all about it before you do it to me, I want you to do it to me and then I'll take your leaflet home.' I wanted the experience first and then the explanation of the experience later. When you become a believer it's like that. You have the experience first: I received him, I believed in him, I committed my way to him, I rested everything I had on him. Now give me the explanation of it. Verse 13 gives you the explanation: you are 'children born not of natural descent, nor of human decision or a husband's will . . .' You *came* to receive him, you *came* to believe in him, because he gave you new birth.

Elohim takes the initiative in the creation and he takes the total initiative in the new creation. So what am I? I am a Christian, a child of God, having received and believed, born of God. I can call him Father. And that brings us to the final point.

What is the key to living life?

The key to living life is how you see yourself. The secularists say there is a way to see yourself, and it is the way of the spiritual derelict. Secularism is spiritual poverty. Don't allow your identity to be defined for you in meaningless ways. How foolish to define yourself by worldly possessions that can be carried away, by those things which will not endure. I am created, I am dependent, I am godlike, I am made for rest in relationship, I am a child of God. That is my identity. Surely one of the great books of the twentieth century is *Knowing God* by Jim Packer. Packer says whenever you have a spare moment in the day, keep saying these six things to yourself. 'I am a child of God. God is my Father; heaven is my home; every day is one day nearer. My Saviour is my brother; every Christian is my brother too.' That's who I am!

2 Humans are breathtaking: Genesis 2:4-25

Introduction

There are some things that we are ignorant about that make absolutely no difference to us, but there are other areas of knowledge which are absolutely fundamental to our maturity. If you are ignorant in these areas, you will be frustrated, confused and ultimately immature, for life. The ignorance I'm talking about is the ignorance that you have of yourself. I was converted in the sixties and at that stage there was a lot of teaching about the Holy Spirit's ministry. In the seventies, to compensate for that, there were a lot of sermon series on the forgotten Fatherhood of God. In the eighties, there seemed to be a great emphasis on the doctrine of the Church. In the nineties there seemed to be an emphasis on the centre of our authority, the Bible, the word of God. But if I was going back into a parish today, the first decade of the twenty-first century, I would spend the first year of my ministry preaching on what the theologians call the doctrine of man and sin: what we believe about ourselves and how we understand the nature of sin.

We've had a knowledge explosion about so many things. It's incredible what we know, and yet we have so little knowledge about ourselves. Yesterday I talked about Calvin's *Institutes of the Christian Religion* and that opening sentence: 'All true wisdom consists of two parts: knowledge of God and knowledge of yourself.' That is what we're dealing with in Genesis 2. We leave behind (v4) the broad sweep of creation; we move from the universe and come to the garden. We move from the proper name of God in Genesis 1, *Elohim*, and now we are introduced to the Creator-God: *Yahweh Elohim*, the covenant-keeping God. In Genesis 1, God is separating light from dark, land from sea: the emphasis in Genesis 2 seems to be the binding together of man and soil, man and woman, man and God.

The first man and the first woman (Gen. 2:4-7)

In this section there are two changes; not only in the name of God, who is now *Yahweh Elohim*, but the focus now is on the perspective of the Earth. Verse 7 has this detailed account of the creation of man (referred to in Genesis 1): 'The LORD God formed the man from the dust of the ground and breathed into his nostrils the breath of life, and the man became a living being.'

The Lord God formed the man, Adam, from the dust of the ground: *adama* is the word for ground. So if we have big thoughts of ourselves, remember that we are formed from the dust. God doesn't just speak something into being: he gets his hands dirty. He forms the man, Adam, from the *adama*: he is carefully, intricately, fearfully and wonderfully made. The dust of the ground is my cradle: it's where I came from. My vocation is to take the dust of the ground and work it and care for it (v15) and it's going to become my grave.[6] For dust you are and to *adama* you will return' (Gen. 3:19).

The emphasis (v7) is that we are just not dust, we are not some mechanical unit. Literally, we are breathtaking. In this intimate way, the Lord God breathes into the nostrils of man. Adam's not some complex combination of chemicals: God animates him with the very breath that animates God. God brings us to life. So in you now there is this eternal element, you are like God, unique in all creation. The breath of God that animates him animates you. We are like God, all of us, everyone on the planet. Everyone is to be respected.

Yahweh Elohim is the great Provider (vs 8–15)

God plants a garden called Eden. Literally it means a place of pleasure and delight. The writer is saying that the garden of Eden is what the Temple and the Tabernacle are going to be like: the place where Yahweh and man will walk together, where they will meet. It's a real place (vs 10–14): notice the place names, the Pishon, the Gihon, the Tigris, the Euphrates. There is an abundant supply of water: this is a place of God's blessing, a place which is well fed.

In the middle of this garden there are two trees (v9): the tree of life and the tree of the knowledge of good and evil. So as man dwells in this garden, he knows immortality: the tree of Life. And right in the middle of this garden is revelation, God revealing his mind and making immortal life accessible to people. Eden is God's. And before the Fall (v15), God took the man and put him in the garden of Eden to work it and take care of it. It's the same word, to work it and care for it, as the service rendered in the Temple or the Tabernacle by the priest. This is a vocation, a calling. God puts him in the garden and says 'Your priestly work is to work the ground and take care of the garden that I am giving to you.' Work is a part of life. It's not a result of the Fall, a punishment. We were created to be productive.

In Australia for the past five or so years we have had a very strong economy. One of the blessings is to have full employment. In Australia, virtually everybody who wants and needs to work can work. In fact, the government is actually paying people to stay in the workforce. And one of the things that troubles me is that whenever we talk about mission, I often hear people say 'This is a great challenge for young people.' Don't believe it! Seventy is the new sixty, eighty is the new seventy. We've got a constant stream of people coming into our college to retrain in their fifties and sixties. We're made to be productive. Unemployment is dehumanising. God says 'You're made to work, so work the ground and take care of the ground.'

God shows care in his warning (Gen. 2:16–17)

'The Lord God commanded the man, "You are free to eat from any tree in the garden, but you must not eat from the tree of the knowledge of good and evil, for when you eat of it, you will surely die."' 'I have your good at heart. I want you to blossom, to flourish, but you will only blossom and flourish as you listen to me and to my word.' God has made us for himself, to walk in the fear of the Lord. To listen to him and reverence him is the essence of the wise person. So what are these ancient words teaching us? That life, direction, growth and fulfilment come to us as we are governed by God's word. He is the Provider who made me. He breathed into me, he placed me in a garden, he gave me work, and he rules. He says do this, but don't do that: it's not in your best interests. The very breath which animates me is the breath which animates him. I work best in relationship with him. What did Augustine say? 'You have made us for thyself, and our hearts are restless until they find their rest in thee.'

Companionship (Gen. 2:18-23)

Then (v18) the God who has said 'that's good, that's good' says 'That's not good.' It is not good for the man to be alone, he needs a suitable helper, a complement, a match. God knows that we are god-like and need companionship. We are more than animals, and so the Lord God caused a deep sleep to fall on Adam and from his rib he creates woman. The first human speech (v23) is ecstatic poetry: 'This is now bone of my bones and flesh of my flesh; she shall be called "woman" for she was taken out of man.' Rough paraphrase: 'I like what I see. She's part of me, she's flesh, she's bone, she's equal, she's my match. She shall be called *Isha* (the Hebrew word) for she was taken out of *Ish*, the man.'

He names her, they are equals, but there is order in the relationship. In Matthew Henry's wonderful words, 'She was taken not from his head to rule over him, nor from his feet to be ruled by him, but she was taken from his side as an equal. She was taken from under his arm for protection, she came from his heart because she is precious to him.' And the woman comes, part of God's care. It's not good to be without her. Marriage is God's usual provision for our need of companionship.

We are building a composite self-image here. What is it that makes us contented? I am created, I am animated by God's breath, I am made in God's image. I am made for relationship with God. The secularist is desperately poor, a victim of his secularism. I am made for the vocation of work, to be ruled, to be guided by God's word, to walk in the fear of the Lord. I am made for companionship. The environment here is perfect, Adam and his wife cannot blame it: 'It's because of the garden of Eden that we ultimately sinned.'

The meaning of marriage (Gen. 2:24–25)

Then God the Provider says (v24), 'For this reason a man will leave his father and mother and be united to his wife, and they will become one flesh.' One of the largest papers in Australia is the

Sydney Morning Herald and recently they surveyed their readers about their aspirations: do you want an adventurous life, a life of recognition, a life of luxury? The vast majority of people responded that they yearned for a stable family life, a solid marriage and a happy family. Governments come and go, and they can define marriage however they like. In Australia, the government in 1974 redefined marriage: 'Marriage is a legal contract between two parties, which can be terminated after twelve months' separation.' Recently, our new Labour government redefined that slightly: 'Marriage is a legal contract between two parties, a man and a woman.' It's positive that they've said that, but there is much more to be said about marriage.

God says, 'For this reason a man will leave his father and mother.' Why is it important for the man to leave his father and mother? Because in Jewish society the man would marry his bride and they would both go and live in his father's house. She goes to live with the in-laws. God says, make sure that a husband leaves his father and mother. You are going to be geographically very close to them but this relationship with your wife is the priority, that comes before a relationship of son to father or mother. 'And they will be united'. The old word is cleave, glued together in this enduring relationship. Feelings of love may come and go, but marriage is not at the mercy of feelings of love. Here is a deep commitment, a union for life. And in that context God says the two will become one flesh.

This is God's plan. He does not say that they will become one flesh, and then, if it works out, be united to one another. The sequencing here is important: the entrance into this relationship is leaving all other relationships one step back, being united to one another and, in that context, becoming one flesh. Marriage in the mind of God is like a three-legged stool: you can't take one or two legs away and still have a stable stool. Living together is taking the gift of marriage without the responsibility of marriage. Here is union, unconditional promises to have and to hold, from this day forward, for better for worse, for richer for poorer, in sickness and in health, to love and to cherish till death do us part.

Safe sex

It is within this lifelong marriage environment that God has placed sex. Safe sex, according to the Bible, according to God, is married sex. It is for life. Sex has become the great addiction of the age, hasn't it? You use someone and discard them. In the act of sex you are saying something with your body to someone that you are not prepared to say with your mind, unless you are in this leaving and cleaving relationship.

The chapter finishes (v25): 'they were both naked.' They express their openness and trust, there was no need to be self-protective. God invented sex, it is a wonderful gift, but it is to be exercised in the right and proper environment, in an enduring lifelong (though not eternal) relationship. It is a uniting, intimate thing. It is God's provision, and it is thoroughly good. It is not a concession to our sinfulness.

God's blueprint in the New Testament

'For this reason a man will leave his father and mother, and he will be united to his wife, and they will become one flesh.' This verse is repeated three more times in the Bible: twice by our Lord Jesus and once by the apostle Paul.

What do Christians believe about marriage?

If someone said to you 'What do Christians uniquely believe about marriage?' you couldn't answer (Genesis 2:24), because Jews believe that as well. But what is it? Paul tells us: 'For this reason (he quotes Genesis) a man will leave his father and mother and be united to his wife and the two will become one flesh' (Eph. 5:31–32). He says this is a profound mystery: the meaning of this has been hidden up to now. What Moses had in mind when he penned these words, inspired by God's Spirit, is not just the husband and the wife but a higher relationship which was to come: the relationship between Jesus and his Church. So what is it that Christians uniquely believe about marriage? We believe that marriage has been elevated to the highest plane. It is a visible representation on Earth of an invisible relationship between Christ and his Church.

The role of husbands and wives

Paul says (v22): 'Wives, submit to your husbands as to the Lord' . . . 'as the church submits to Christ so wives should submit to their husbands in everything' (v24). In other words, the wife is to look to the Church for her model, to respect her husband and submit.

Husbands, on the other hand, are to 'love your wives, just as Christ loved the church and gave himself up for her' (v25). The love of Christ is present, continuous, ongoing. The love of Christ for the Church makes the Church the object of every verb here, and so the husband is to make the wife the object of every verb. Verses 26–27: 'to make her holy, cleansing her by the washing with water through the word, and to present her to himself as a radiant church, without stain or wrinkle or any other blemish, but holy and blameless.' Husbands, look to the Lord Jesus. Wives, look to the Church. Look at that husband and wife – it reminds me of Jesus and the Church.

So when my three new sons-in-law came to me and asked my permission to marry our daughters, I had a number of questions for them. 'Can you love my daughter for the rest of your life?' And speaking to my daughters about their intendeds: 'Can you respect him for the rest of your life?' Marriage points away from itself, it is in this sense sacramental. That's what Christians believe about marriage: it's not a concession, it's a wonderful thing! It reminds me of Jesus and the Church.

Singleness also is a wonderful thing. Singleness gives us a glimpse into heaven as well, because there is no marriage in heaven. The person who is living in the freedom of celibate singleness is able to mix widely, become a member of many families; to give themselves in a single-minded way; to serve widely in a way which may not be appropriate for the married person.

So what went wrong?

There it is, the Eden paradise, mankind from the hand of God, energised by his breath, absolutely dependent, a steward having governance over the garden and companionship in a lifelong covenant relationship with one another. Yahweh is a God who enters into the covenant with us and so we are covenant-making and keeping beings who are morally accountable, designed at every point to have reference to God. I am most human when I am most God-focused; most contented when I know that I am loved by him, and I follow him. At the end of a chapter we have this wonderful picture. We are breathtaking. Aspiring to live like angels, consenting to live like apes.

What happened? How did we lose it all? Is there some way back? Nikita Khrushchev, head of the Soviet Union in the 1960s, said 'Communism's failure was its failure to produce the selfless man.' Politics has got no answer for us. We need to understand our predicament first.

God the great Diagnostician

He will tell us how we got to where we are, and how we get back. In Romans 1, Paul talks about the predicament of mankind. He says 'For although they knew God, they neither glorified him as God nor gave thanks to him, but their thinking became futile and their foolish hearts were darkened' (Rom. 1:21). The appropriate response to God is to glorify him and to give him thanks. But the wrath of God is being revealed against our godlessness and our wickedness (v18). Humankind made this exchange (v23): they 'exchanged the glory of the immortal God for images made to look like mortal man and birds and animals and reptiles.' They exchanged the truth of God literally for this lie: they 'worshipped and served created things rather than the Creator – who is for ever praised. Amen' (v25).

This is our problem

Every element of creation in Genesis 1, at some time in the history of humankind, has been worshipped by people. That is the great lie: to take that which God has created, and turn it into the creator, as though it is to be worshipped. Instead of glorifying and giving him thanks, we have become godless and wicked, without excuse (v20): 'For since the creation of the world God's invisible qualities – his eternal power and his divine nature – have been clearly seen, being understood from what has been made, so that men are without excuse.' The revelation of God is there in the created order: and yet instead of recognising and giving him thanks, we have turned to godlessness and wickedness. That's the problem, Paul says.

God gave them over

So what has God done? He's given us over (vs 24, 26, 28). He says 'I'll give you up to the fruit of idolatry.' It is the hidden wrath of God (v24): what you will have is all forms of uncleanness. 'God gave them over to shameful lusts. Even their women exchanged natural relations for unnatural ones' (v26). God 'gave them over to a depraved mind to do what ought not to be done . . . They are gossips, slanderers, God-haters, insolent' (v28,30). 'They are senseless, faithless, heartless, ruthless' (v31). God gave them up. And in all of this they are passionate to make converts to depravity . . . 'although they know God's righteous decree that those who do such things deserve death, they not only continue to do these very things but also approve of those who practise them' (v32).

Why did God give them over? Because they came into contact with God's revelation of himself, God's eternal power and divine nature, and they turned away from it to the great lie of idolatry. That is why we are the way we are.

What is our diagnosis?

We have a deeply ingrained theological infection: we have turned away from the revelation of God and we have worshipped the created order. What antibiotic can you apply to this infection which will be effective in defeating it? A theological infection demands a theological antibiotic. The only antibiotic which will work is the gospel of the Lord Jesus. That alone will bring us back into what we were meant to be, into relationship with God. Life is torn and perverted and out of shape. We try everything else, but we don't try God and his great gospel, and yet that will bring us back. Only the gospel can take people with a marred image and restore us through new birth for life in the new creation.

A changed man

I was seventeen years of age, growing up in a home where Christianity was mocked and Christians were teased, and I'll never forget the day my father, a fifty-year old man, came into my bedroom and said 'I've become a Christian.' 'You are kidding!' I said. He said 'I've been a good father and I've never asked much of you. I want you to come to church with me.' I watched him. I used to buy his cigarettes for him; I poured his beers for him. I never poured another beer! I never bought another cigarette! He didn't become a perfect man but he became a changed man.

I haven't got all the answers to life, but I know the only one who had the right to stay in the Garden of Eden didn't stay there. He came to this planet so that those who received him might have the right to heaven and the Tree of Life. You can have the foretaste now, and a certain expectation one day of re-entry. And in knowing him, my father came to know himself. It's simple, but it's not simplistic. Tell him you're sorry, then say please and thank you. I'm sorry I've ignored you, Yahweh. Thank you for sending Jesus for me. Please rule my life by your loving word.

Do you know who you are?

3 From nude to shrewd: Genesis 3:1–13

Introduction

In Australia we have a concerted, government-funded anti-smoking campaign, and some of those advertisements are shockingly confronting. I think the most effective that I have seen is the advertisement that asks the question 'If a cigarette was your friend, what sort of a friend would it be? It drives you out late at night to pick up some more. It separates you from your mates; you have to go outside to smoke. It takes a hundred dollars from your pocket every week. And in the end it will kill you. If a cigarette was your friend, what sort of a friend would it be?'

The advertising executive who dreamt up that question 'If a cigarette was your friend what sort of a friend would it be?' must have been reading Paul in Romans 8, because he asks exactly that question. 'If your sin nature was your friend, what sort of a friend would it be?' What obligation do you have to your sin nature? When did your sin nature ever do anything for you that you were proud of? When was the last time you gave in to temptation and felt 'That was good'? So, the apostle Paul says, why do you keep investing in your sinful nature? That leads us today to Genesis 3, the first mention of sin. It is simple, clear and devastatingly destructive.

Two conversations (Gen. 3:1–7)

The first one is between the serpent and Eve (vs 1-5). He suddenly appears: there's no explanation for him but we know where he comes from, when we read the book of Revelation. All we are told in verse one is that he is crafty, and the link is with chapter 2:25. I've used the words nude and shrewd because they rhyme in

English, but in Hebrew the word 'naked' in verse 25 and the word 'crafty' in chapter 3:1 is exactly the same word. Here were the man and his wife, they were naked. But they yearned for more than that. They were not happy to be nude, they wanted also to add shrewd. Jesus said it's good to be as shrewd as a serpent and as gentle as a dove, but the serpent takes this shrewdness and uses it in an anti-God way.

How does his shrewdness show itself? (v1)

The serpent goes to the woman. That's not a sexist statement: it's a statement of reality. He goes to the woman to ask her about a conversation in which she was not a part. It was a conversation which Yahweh Elohim had with Adam. The woman wasn't even created, yet the serpent asks her about the details of this conversation. Notice what he says: he stresses the prohibition: 'Did God really say "You must not eat from any tree in the garden"?'

He refers to God as God, not as the LORD God. He's got no time for Yahweh, the covenant-keeping faithful God, he just gives him his proper name, Elohim. Let's remind ourselves of what God did say: 'And the LORD God commanded the man, "You are free to eat from any tree in the garden, but you must not eat from the tree of the knowledge of good and evil, for when you eat of it you will surely die."'

Notice how the woman responds (vs 2,3). She corrects the serpent but in a way which sides with him. She says 'We may eat fruit from the trees in the garden'. That's true, but she adds to the prohibition as if to show that it is really unreasonable and overbearing: she says 'He said we shouldn't eat it or touch it.' God said nothing about not touching it.

What should she have done? In Australian sport you are always taught to think with the mind of the opposing captain and then do the opposite. The serpent wanted her to enter into a conversation about another conversation which she really didn't know about firsthand. What should she have done? 'You know so much, serpent, go and talk to God. Or, my husband was there, go and talk to him.' No, she takes it on herself to talk to him.

'You will not surely die' (vs 4,5)

'You will not surely die,' he says, and he questions God's motivation. 'Don't you realise that he's only trying to protect his Godness?' The Devil is telling a half truth at this point. It's not going to be immediately lethal: Adam lived for 930 years after he ate the fruit from the tree. But the Devil is showing one of his strategies: he specialises in telling a half truth, and when a half truth is told as though it were the full truth it is actually an untruth. You won't die immediately, but the full truth is that the process of death will inevitably begin, and physical death will follow.

The Devil is saying (v5), 'God knows that when you eat of it, your eyes will be opened, and you will be like God, knowing good and evil.' He doesn't want that sort of competition, he doesn't want to share his Godness with you. He doesn't have your best interests at heart. It's a half truth.

The devastatingly destructive result (vs 6,7)

The woman lets her senses be her guide, and we read 'she took some and she ate it. She also gave it to her husband and he ate it.' Whenever your senses or emotions collide with reason, generally they win out. It reminds me of David and Bathsheba. He saw her taking a bath, he sent for her, she came to him, he slept with her, and she left. What the woman is saying is 'I know this is his garden, his rule, but I will launch myself out and declare my humanness.' That's what sin does.

Look at the immediate result (v7); 'the eyes of both of them were opened and they realised they were naked; so they sewed fig leaves together and made coverings for themselves.' In Genesis 2:25, the man and his wife were naked and they felt no shame. Then look at chapter 3:8, there's a great contrast: 'Then the man and his wife heard the sound of the LORD God as he was walking in the garden in the cool of the day and they hid'. They wanted to cover up, and this is the effect of sin.

The second conversation (vs 8-13)

'The LORD God called to the man, "Where are you?"' Didn't he know where Adam was? Of course he did. It's exactly the same when he calls to Cain in chapter 4, 'Where is your brother Abel?' God knew very well where he was but he wants Cain to have the opportunity to confess what he has done. He is a just judge, he doesn't jump to conclusions. He gives Adam the opportunity to confess. He says 'I heard you in the garden, and I was afraid because I was naked.' 'Who told you you were naked? Have you eaten from the tree?' And the man says 'The woman you put here with me . . . She did it.'

There's a radical change taking place here. The essence of the being of Yahweh, the covenant-keeping God, is faithfulness. The essence of the being of the serpent is lies. John says in the book of Revelation that the other great dominating characteristic of the Devil is that he accuses the brethren. So you find those two characteristics in the man's response. He lies, and then he accuses. Then the woman says 'The serpent gave it to me. The serpent deceived me and I ate it.' The poor old serpent's got no one else to blame. The accusation indicates that Adam and his wife have gone over to the other side. They now bear the very characteristics not of their Father the Creator God but the serpent. They have moved to his camp. Friends, every funeral you have been to since is a sacramental reminder that sin has come into the world.

You know immediately when you see a dysfunctional relationship. A person comes out and kicks their pet dog. A parent in a supermarket just lets it all go and slaps and slaps their child who is having a tantrum. God says they can have the fruit of any of the trees but that one, and Adam and his wife disregard his word. When do you find the relationship becomes a model relationship? Flip over to Genesis 15. If this is a dysfunctional relationship, where is the functional relationship? Look at verse 4. Remember the context here is the Lord Yahweh speaking to Abram, and he makes a promise: 'Then the word of the LORD came to him'. He promises that as the stars in the heavens, 'so shall your offspring be' (v6). 'Abram believed the Lord, and he credited it to him as righteousness.' Here is the model. God speaks his word, Abram believes the word of God, and it is credited as righteousness, he receives God's tick of approval. Here is the functional relationship, as it was meant to be: Yahweh speaks, we believe and trust. That's the pattern which Adam and his wife have broken.

A crafty adversary

You have an enemy. He is real, he is spiritual, and he is present. Your battle is not against people, against flesh and blood. It's against the evil behind the flesh and blood: the serpent. Where did he come from? He came from the heavenly court. Revelation says that he was an angel and Michael and his angels cast him down to the Earth where he has a limited timespan. What is he like? Peter says he's like a roaring lion, seeking someone to devour.

Take it seriously. His strategy is to tell you a half truth as though it were the full truth and that is an untruth. One of our daughters and her husband are missionaries in Mongolia. The Mongolian Church is a very young church. There were one or two believers when the first missionaries got in and today the Church consists of between thirty and forty thousand believers. Most of these people grew up in the Soviet time and they were tutored never to trust anyone, because you didn't know if you were speaking to a Soviet spy.

The greatest threat to the Mongolian Church today is people, like me, who go and visit for a weekend, and tell them a half truth as though it were a full truth, and it's a lie and an untruth. My son-in-law said, 'We see them come in from overseas and they preach a tantalising message – you come to Jesus and you can have health and wealth beyond your dreams.' It's a half truth. God said, in the old covenant, 'Be faithful to me and I'll see that you have good harvests.' But there's no place here for suffering. Isn't it interesting that James says 'Count it pure joy my brethren, when you suffer trials of many kinds.' He was giving them a developed doctrine of suffering because they had been tutored and discipled to understand suffering in the New Testament age, but we don't give anybody an understanding of how to suffer. 'Come to Jesus and he'll give you health and wealth!' In the new covenant, those blessings become spiritual blessings of forgiveness and the Holy Spirit. And these people come to Christ expecting wealth. They have been told not to trust anyone, and so they ask, 'Can we trust the Christian God?' And so eventually, they say, 'Of course we can't, he didn't make us wealthy. We've tried Christianity.' And they leave the Church. Because of people like me, who go out and present a half truth as though it were the full truth. It is a devilish satanic untruth. And where will he end up? In the lake of fire. He is a lame duck, but he is active. Don't focus on him, be aware of him.

Sin is the destination of which temptation is the route

Don't let your senses be your guide. The only way to beat temptation, someone said, is with your hat. Grab it and run. I think we live in an age where we trivialise sin. It is serious. It's going to take the blood of God's own Son to deal with this problem. Do you have an awareness of your own sinfulness? Are you repenting continually? That's the drainage system of the soul. Are you turning back to God continually?

Recently I was at a houseparty, giving talks, and the pastor asked me to move amongst the various Bible study groups which met after my talk. There was a whole range of people from the very elderly to the quite young, all doing the same Bible study. And I vividly remember sitting in a group of about a dozen young people, all university or post-university age. They'd been very well discipled. They were biblically literate and theologically astute, and the group was very well led. This was the question: how can we resist temptation more effectively? And these were the answers: we need to absorb the Bible, to delight in God's word and to reflect on it day and night. That's true. We need to pray more for God's strength: that's true. We need to make ourselves accountable to one another: that's true. Anything else? Not another thing. Not one person mentioned the Person of the Holy Spirit. Does he have some relevance to us? Have we lost our awareness of him? Have we lost our confidence in him? It is he who leads us to resist the process of temptation.

Flip over in your Bible to Romans 8. In this chapter the apostle Paul's theme is Christian maturity. He has more references in Romans 8 to the Holy Spirit than in all of the other combined parts of the whole letter. This is what he says in Romans 8:14: 'Those who are led by the Spirit of God are sons of God.' An incredible truth, isn't it? We often use that expression 'the Spirit led me to marry this man or this woman, the Spirit led me to this vocation, the Spirit led me to be a missionary in this country' but that's not the way the Bible uses that term. Paul uses that term, the Spirit leading, here and in Galatians, and always in the context of the Spirit leading to say no to sin. Verse thirteen gives the context; 'If you live according to the sinful nature, you will die, but if by the Spirit you put to death the misdeeds of the body, you will live.' So I'm absolutely dependent upon the Holy Spirit to say no to the sinful nature, and therefore I need to have more awareness of him and more confidence in him. Recently the Deputy Secretary of State of the United States visited Australia and was asked about the ongoing battle against terrorism. He said to the interviewer 'Do you realise that every day in which there is no incident is really a day of great victory for us? Because it means that our systems are working.'

I think the advice I have to give students more commonly than anything else is don't be self accusing. That's the Devil's work, don't help him in that! Have more confidence in the Holy Spirit. Recognise that today you have had significant victories in your Christian walk. And it is you, in the power of the Spirit, dying to your sinful nature. Currently in Sydney outside a number of churches there's a sign, and it says 'This church is full of hypocrites. There's room for one more.' It's disturbing, isn't it? It's like the sign people put on the back of their car 'Christians aren't perfect, just forgiven.' It makes me uneasy. Should I feel comfortable with my hypocrisy? Should I just learn to live with my imperfection?

I think we are in a state in the history of the Church where we've seen some of the extreme emphases of the Neo-Pentecostal movement, and we have lost our awareness of the Holy Spirit of God in our own lives. We've heard about Christian perfectionism and we're becoming too accepting of the sin that is within. There's a battle going on and we need to resist in the power of the Holy Spirit. Paul, when he wrote to Titus, said that Jesus 'gave himself for us to redeem us from all wickedness' – that's behind – 'and to purify for himself a people that are his very own.' It's the same thing twice. He came to purify you for himself: a people who belong to him, who are zealous for good deeds. Put it behind you. Have you forgotten that when you came to Christ, you came under the agency of the Holy Spirit, your sin was forgiven, he baptised you into Christ and he now fills you? That's where our confidence lies. Yes, we have a subtle, awful enemy. But we have a more than adequate friend, the Paraclete of God himself.

We need to recognise what sin is

Sin is a dreadful thing, it is cosmic treason against heaven's King. Notice the order of things in Genesis 1 and 2: we are introduced to God, who speaks to man, who speaks to woman and who rules the created order. Get that order: God, man, woman, creation. When you come to Genesis 3, you have creation, the serpent, speaking to the woman, who speaks to the man, who speaks to God. You have this reversal of the normal order, that is why sin is cosmic treason. It's like taking the creation and de-creating it, turning it upside down. Sin is self assertion, sin is Adam and his wife shaking their fists at God and saying No! And it represents a fundamental rebellion against him.

Is there any hope? Go back to chapter 3 of Genesis. There are just three words that indicate hope to us: 'But the LORD God called to the man, "Where are you?"'

When my dad was converted, I was determined that I wasn't going to be converted. I was going to take up his mantle and tease Christians. Trouble is, I was playing in a tennis team and the captain of the tennis team happened to be a Christian and invited me along to a church houseparty for young people. And so I went. The day before I went, I bought myself a pipe. I thought, I'll mock these Christians, I'll blow pipe smoke over their Bible studies. And I did, Saturday, all day. Sunday morning I went down to breakfast as a mocker and teaser of Christians, and then Sunday lunch I came to lunch as a man who had found God's grace absolutely irresistible.

I had heard a man talk about Malachi. He challenged me with the gospel. I'd never known anything about that. And I'd heard about this Yahweh Elohim, who came for me, in all my self-righteous rebellion and said 'Where are *you*?' I couldn't resist it! Yahweh Elohim cannot help himself. 'Where are you' in the face of rebellion and resistance. His outgoing generous grace: 'Where are you?' His grace is irresistible. But the Lord God, Yahweh Elohim, called to this man who had taken from his wife in clear rebellion, and eaten and now is hiding away from him: 'Where are you? What have you done? Talk to me. Where are you?'

Abraham: Covenant, creation and chaos

by Liam Goligher

Liam Goligher

Liam has been Senior Pastor of Duke Street Church in Richmond since April 2000. He has also pastored churches in Ireland, Canada and in his native Scotland. His teaching is heard weekly on Premier Radio, Sky Digital and Freeview. His Duke Street ministry is also available online. Liam has contributed to a number of books, as well as writing three of his own: *Window On Tomorrow, The Fellowship of the King* and most recently *The Jesus Gospel*. He is married to Christine, and they have five children, three grand-daughters and a Bedlington terrier.

1 Believing God: Genesis 15 – 17

Introduction

These three chapters are a teaching unit; bracketed by this whole idea of a 'covenant'. In the Old Testament, the word 'covenant' is used for the intimacy of the relationship God has with his people. When God started to communicate with humans, he selected a method, the covenant, that was known to them from the area of international relations.

What is a covenant?

It's one of those words that reoccurs in the Bible. There are those who feel this is one of the biggest ideas in the Bible, perhaps even the organising idea. Certainly it's important to Christians, because at the Lord's Supper we drink the cup of the new covenant; and this covenant with Abram is important to God. There are other covenants in the Bible, such as the covenant with Moses, but nowhere do you find in the subsequent history of Israel that God ever comes to his people and says, 'Remember the covenant that I made with Moses.' Whenever God wants to reassure his people, he always says, 'Remember the covenant I made with Abraham.' This covenant of promise is vital to an understanding of the big storyline of the Bible as a whole.

The idea of a covenant is both formal and familiar; relational and legal. It points to an agreement between a greater and a lesser, and there are two kinds of covenant that are reflected in the Bible. One is known as a 'suzerainty treaty', and the other is known as a 'royal grant'. A suzerainty treaty has to do with an overlord and his vassal, while a royal grant involves the same parties but has a slightly different connotation. The first is conditional: it imposes obligations and has the threat of curses and the promise of blessing. The second is unconditional: it bestows gifts and announces a promise. Let me illustrate these two to you.

A suzerainty treaty

It's a relational arrangement. Usually the big king, the overlord, was called the father of the people, so there was a relationship involved. Normally when a covenant was drawn up, there was a preamble identifying who the overlord was, then there was a historic prologue that recited the relationship between the overlord and the little king, and then there were stipulations: sanctions for violation or blessings for obedience. Perhaps the simplest one is found in Genesis 1–2. In Genesis 1, you have an introduction to God: the overlord. He is the one who owns the territory. In chapter 2, you have a repetition of the story of the making of humanity. This is the historical prologue reminding us of the particular relationship between the big king, God, and the little king, Adam. In Genesis 2 there are also stipulations: one rule – but there is a curse for its violation and an implied promise for obedience. If Adam and Eve obey God's word, they'll stay in the land, in Eden, and enjoy God's company there.

So a suzerainty treaty is a covenant of law, it always involves an obligation, and there are always sanctions for violation. The books of Moses, Genesis to Deuteronomy, begin and end with suzerainty treaties. There's the one in Eden and the one with Israel in Canaan. When the children of Israel were listening to Moses teaching this, they would realise immediately that Adam was on probation in Eden, just as they were going to be in Canaan. Just as they had been tested in the wilderness and failed, so Adam had been tested in the Garden and failed. In Matthew's gospel, Jesus comes as the new

Israel: called out of Egypt, tested in the wilderness and then, at the end of his ministry in a rerun of Eden, he's tested in the Garden and, as the new Adam, the new Israel, he succeeds. He obeys where they disobeyed. And as a result of his obedience, you get to the end of Matthew and Jesus says, 'All authority in heaven and on earth has been given to me.'

A royal grant

This was a gift bestowed by a great king on his vassal. It was usually one-sided: there were no stipulations and no sanctions; it was an outright gift by a king to his subject. It was eternal rather than temporary and did not put anyone on probation, as these other covenants did. It was a covenant of promise, of grace. The promise made to Adam in Genesis 3:15, the covenants made with Noah, Abram, and David and the new covenant – these are all royal grants, given as free gifts by God.

The promise-maker

God appeared to Abram in a vision. It wasn't what he *saw* that gripped him so much as what he *heard*: he heard God speak. The promise-maker is the Lord who says to him: 'Fear not, Abram, I am your shield, your reward shall be very great.' Here's the formula God is going to use when he comes to Moses and introduces himself: 'I am that I am.' Later still, the Lord Jesus, when he comes in the flesh into the world, declares over and over again: 'I am. Before Abram was, I am.'

What is the reward that God gives to Abram? Himself: '*I am* your shield. *I am* the reward. The great gift *I am* giving to you is myself.' And it's still the case for the believer, wherever we are, that the greatest treasure that God gives to us is himself. He will be a God to us: that is the promise that God is giving this man. He is bestowing this royal gift on a servant. He will be both his Defender against foreign hostile forces, and his Benefactor who will ensure an inheritance in the future. And that is the promise that Abram believes. He may go on to doubt and stumble, but he believes God and that becomes the vital part of the story.

Liam Goligher

God makes this great promise to him (v2) and Abram starts complaining. Abram says, 'I continue childless.' He's saying to God, 'Thank you for making this promise, which you made quite a considerable time ago, but I don't see any evidence yet of this gift of offspring.'

He's heard this promise before, and he's now looking for the son in fulfilment of God's word. Even his complaint was a complaint of faith (v6). Whenever you have big questions about what's going on, spread them out before the Lord. Abram brings the matter that's on his mind before the Lord, and the Lord answers him (v4): 'Your very own son shall be your heir.'

God is not arguing, he's revealing something to Abram. The heir will not be a distant relative, it will be 'your very own son'. Remember those words, because Abram's going to take them very literally and seriously in the future. Here is the promise of God going a little bit further, and it emphasises and illustrates the fact that what is on Abram's mind at this point is the offspring. God had made three promises to him: about the seed (or offspring), about the land and the blessing. Being a blessing to people was a good thing, getting the land was fine, but the real thing that was on his mind was the promise of the Man-child, the Saviour seed who was going to come into the world. That was the blessing of humanity, and that's what he's focussing on. So God brings him outside (v5) and says to him, 'Look up at the sky there, what do you see? Number the stars if you are able to.' 'So shall your offspring be.' Abram looks at the sky with all the stars, the word of God ringing in his ears. Here's an amazing assurance of God's creative, sovereign power and God's promise to this man.

The promise-believer

Awed by this promise and standing under the stars, looking at God's picture book painting of the future of his people, Abram responded. He believed the Lord (v6) and the Lord 'counted it to Abram as righteousness.' God's word became the ground upon which he stood. Here is a landmark principle from the Bible's revelation of God's dealings with people: it will be this principle that will be unpacked in the rest of the Bible. God speaks, Abram believes God. On the basis of his establishing this covenant arrangement, unilaterally and unconditionally, Abram is justified. Here is a constant principle – this is the way it's going to work in these covenant relationships with God. This is, forever more, going to be the basis of the way in which a person enjoys an intimate, ongoing and eternal relationship with God.

When Moses says Abram believed the Lord, he's telling us that he put his trust in God to keep his promises. Wherever Moses uses the word 'to believe', on every occasion it has to do with confidence in the reliability of God. Believing became the characteristic of Abram's relationship with God. He was a believer, from this point on.

What specifically did Abram believe?

This is an important question. Is this passage simply teaching us that God justifies people who just believe? Is it just believing generally, or is there something he believed that made the difference? If you look at the context, Abram's response to God's promise makes it clear that the emphasis in this section is on the offspring. In the previous section, chapters 12–14, the emphasis is on the land. In chapters 15–17, the focus is on the offspring, the seed. So he's believing in the promise of the offspring that was first promised to Adam and Eve in the Garden. That is a promise about Jesus, the coming Messiah. What did Abram believe? He believed in the promise about Christ. He was saved by looking forward to Jesus, in the same way that we are saved by looking back to Jesus.

What does it mean to be recognised as righteous?

Because Abram believed in this Saviour, he was counted as righteous. The people who were listening to Moses as he preached this to them were familiar with the law of Moses, and they understood very well that, in the law of Moses, to be regarded as righteous you had to keep the law. Wherever this word righteousness is used normally, it is credited to someone on the basis of what they *do*. Here's the point of

Genesis 15: a declaration that would normally be declared on the basis of what one *does*, is here granted to Abram on the basis of the fact that he *believes* God. This would have jarred in the minds of these people. In the desert, the covenant of Moses was a covenant of law. If you keep the law, if you do all these things, then you'll be righteous. But here's God declaring Abram righteous on the basis of the fact he believes God. If God declares Abram righteous, it means God himself views Abram as righteous; not on the basis of what he does but on the basis of his faith. If you think that's pushing it, let me give you the apostolic exposition of this passage in Romans 4

> What then shall we say was gained by Abraham, our forefather according to the flesh? For if Abraham was justified by works, he has something to boast about, but not before God. For what does the Scripture say? "Abraham believed God, and it was counted to him as righteousness." Now to the one who works, his wages are not counted as a gift but as his due. And to the one who does not work but believes in him who justifies the ungodly, his faith is counted as righteousness (Rom. 4:1–5).

Paul is arguing that before the law of Moses was even given, going right back as far as we can go, our right relationship with God was always about faith in Christ. Christ in promise, perhaps, but in Christ nonetheless.

This word 'counted' is a good word. It was used of the Levite (Num. 18:27–28): 'your contribution shall be counted to you as though it were the grain of the threshing floor, and as the fullness of the winepress. So you shall also present a contribution to the LORD from all your tithes, which you receive from the people of Israel.' The law said to take everything you grew and to give a tithe of it to God, but the Levites didn't grow anything. God is saying, 'I know that you haven't grown anything, but when you tithe from what they give to you in their tithe, your tithe will be counted as if it was something you'd grown.' That's the use of the word here. For Abram, it was the promise of God that looked forward to Jesus. For us, it's specifically believing in the promise of Christ who has fulfilled all God's promises.

The promise-keeper

Abram believed God and he asked for a sign. We've seen that a covenant was a common form of agreement, and I've mentioned two different kinds of covenant. The other thing about these covenants, whatever kind they were, is that normally those making them would engage in some rituals. They would make the covenant by virtue of these rituals. Normally there were some sacrifices and the carcasses were torn up. Then promises were made and curses were sworn, that would be enacted if anyone should break the terms of the covenant.

In this covenant, things are different. Everything goes according to plan at first, because Abram is told to prepare a variety of sacrificial animals. Here we have Abram adding something else to his CV; we've seen him acting as a king and a prophet, now he's acting as a priest, getting everything ready for the sacrifice. But when it comes to it actually being established, Abram is sound asleep (v12): 'As the sun was going down, a deep sleep fell on Abram. And behold, dreadful and great darkness fell upon him.' The people with Moses would remember the terrifying night at Sinai. Some of them would remember the stories of the people who had actually left Egypt, and the night of the Passover, when a great darkness fell over Egypt on minds go forward in history two thousand years to Calvary, where a darkness came on the face of the Earth at midday for three hours. And in the darkness, a flaming torch resembling the flame of God's splendour and glory walks through the severed halves. Here is God making the covenant by himself, walking between the severed pieces, assuming on his own head the covenant curses should it fail to come to pass. Here is a unilateral promise being sealed by a unilateral treaty ceremony: it is a one-sided promise. God does all the work.

Here is God saying to Abram, 'I would rather die than my covenant promise to you be broken, to fail humanity by not providing the man I have promised to humanity.' So the promise is sealed by sacrifice, echoed by the sacrifices at Sinai and beyond; ultimately echoed by the work of Jesus on our behalf. For how could the living God ever undertake to experience the curses due to human-ity's failure to fulfil our part of the bargain? Only if God took on human flesh and came into the world would he take responsibility for our human sin in human skin. It was to take the God-man, the Saviour seed, going to the cross and taking on the curse there.

The promise-defeater

Chapter 16 tells the story of the typically human effort to help God out by bringing the promise to pass by man's wisdom rather than by God's purpose. It's the story of Sarah and Hagar. Sarah, Abram's wife, has borne him no children and, as they're talking about the promise that God has made, Sarah says to Abram, 'When God was speaking to you, he said it would be your very own son that would be the promise bearer?' Abram says, 'Yes.' 'So he didn't say it would be "your and Sarah's very own son?"' 'No, he didn't say that.' 'Because, if you bear that detail in mind, there's a way we can make this happen.'

It was the custom that if a woman was barren she could take her servant girl and use her as a surrogate to bear a child for her. Sarah comes up with this idea, and it must have sounded very plausible to Abram. Sarah and Abram were trying to short circuit God's promise. They were tired of waiting. She had in her mind that Hagar would have a child, Hagar would go back to doing the dishes, and Sarah would bring the child up as her own. Some of us can't wait for God to keep his promises. That's one of the lies of the health, wealth and prosperity teaching: we can't wait. We can't wait for heaven, for glory, we want what God has for us, now.

In his impatience, Abram takes matters into his own hands. Having been justified by faith, he's now trying to live by works. He's doing some-thing culturally acceptable in those days, but it is a denial of the one flesh principle of creation, and the result is predictable: Hagar becomes preg-nant, has a son and becomes arrogant. Sarah feels despised, she makes life miserable for Hagar, Hagar makes life miserable for Sarah. It all comes to grief. Sarah turns on Abram and blames him (v5). Abram bats it right back to her and, in the ensuing tension, Hagar runs off into the desert.

Who is to blame? It's never straightforward. Each one has sinned against the other. Hagar heads for Egypt, desolate. She runs from the one place on the Earth where God can bless her, and yet it's the chosen family who have pushed her away. How many people are running away from God today because the chosen family have pushed them away? In her misery, God comes to her. The point of the story is that Abram tried to do things his way, and sin always complicates things. The mess started when Abram took measures into his own hands.

Paul uses this story in Galatians 4 as an illustration of the difference between faith and works, Sinai and Jerusalem, law and promise. He says Hagar the slave and Sarah the free woman illustrate two different roots to finding God's salvation. One is a religion of law, of doing what you can do to achieve the goal. The other is the religion of promise that waits for God to give the inheritance in his own time. Paul argues that the promise-defeater is when you start to turn faith into works, when you turn your relationship with God from that based upon promise to that based upon performance. That defeats the promise.

The promise-marker

This time God makes it very clear that it's Sarah who will bear the child. Chapter 16 ends with Abram 86 years old, Chapter 17 starts and Abram is 99 years old. We are taught again that faith often has to wait: it's not always easy to believe. Throughout all of those years Abram had to live with the embarrassment of his name. It meant 'exalted father'. In that context, in chapter 17, God says 'I am God Almighty. My covenant is with you, and you shall be the father of a multitude of nations. No longer shall your name be called Abram, exalted father, but Abraham, father of a multitude of nations.'

Abraham is also told that his relationship with God is going to be everlasting; God's never going to break it. The new promise that God gives to Abraham is repeated through Jeremiah and then in the new covenant, and it's planted in the heart of every believer: 'I will be a

God to you.' God gives them a sign of the covenant: circumcision is to be the mark that identifies those who share the promise with God. Covenant signs are not a sign of our commitment to God, but of God's commitment to us. The sacraments are a covenant sign that reassures the faith of believing people. Abram takes God's words seriously and he becomes Abraham, the father of many nations.

God was serious: 'After this I looked, and behold, a great multitude that no one could number, from every nation, from all tribes and peoples and languages, standing before the throne and before the Lamb.' They're all children of Abraham. As I look around this room today, I see some of Abraham's family here, because God kept his promise. If you believe in Jesus, you become Abraham's offspring.

2 God's friend: Genesis 18 – 19

Introduction

Abraham is the only person in the Bible who is called God's friend. He's called that three times: in Chronicles, Isaiah and in James. Abraham wasn't perfect: he often got things wrong and had to live with his mistakes, as we do, but he's called God's friend, and in chapters 18 and 19, we find their friendship at work.

These two chapters hang together by a number of clear threads. For example, there are two angelic visits: one to Abraham (18) and one to Lot (19). There's a contrast between the visit at noonday (18) and at night time (19). When the angels arrive, Abraham is sitting at the door of his tent: when they arrive in Sodom, Lot is sitting at the gate of the city. In both chapters, visitors arrive, greetings are given and a meal is served. In chapter 18, there is a threat of judgement on Sodom and in chapter 19 there is an outpouring of judgement on Sodom. In chapter 18 there's an intercession by Abraham on behalf of Sodom, and in chapter 19:29, there is the indication that the salvation of Lot from Sodom is dependent on the intercession of Abraham. 'So it was that, when God destroyed the cities of the valley, God remembered Abraham and sent Lot out of the midst of the overthrow when he overthrew the cities in which Lot had lived.'

These two chapters are going to highlight the relationship that exists between Abraham and God. Yesterday, we looked at chapter 17 and we saw the covenant ceremony in two parts. We saw God making his covenant with Abraham, confirming it by the sacrificial system, then repeating the covenant and instituting the mark of the covenant; the rite of circumcision. Now God comes to Abraham again. And the star of the show in chapters 18 and 19 is God himself.

God the faithful and true (Gen. 18:1–15)

It starts off with these visitors turning up in the middle of the day at high noon to Abraham's tent. It was Yahweh who appeared to him by the oaks of Mamre. No doubt Abraham was sitting out there, the way you sit outside your tent if you're down in the South of France camping and it gets to 43 degrees. Slumber has come across you, when suddenly three strangers appear out of nowhere. He doesn't see them coming on the horizon, they just appear. And he immediately springs into action. The language is hurried: he hurried, he went quickly, he ran. It's quite interesting, the language which he uses. He invites them to stay for a morsel of bread, that they might refresh themselves. So he offers them a sandwich, but he gives them a four course meal. He serves the meal himself and, (v8) he stands over them, ready to jump to attention, ready to serve them while they eat. It's a great picture of Eastern hospitality.

It's unclear at what point Abraham realises it's the Lord. Moses tells us at the beginning that it was the Lord. The fact that they arrive unexpectedly is an indication that it's the Lord. The word that Abraham uses, 'Lord', is actually an unusual word to use for 'sir' or a formal word for 'lord' (with a lower case 'l'). It's a word that is normally used for God, though it may very well be used in an ordinary way here.

However we interpret that, there's no doubt that what we have here is a visitation by the second Person of the Godhead. Whenever God appears to people in the Old Testament, it is always the second Person of the Godhead who appears. This is a pre-incarnate appearance of the Son, the one through whom the Godhead interacts with humanity in the Old Testament.

This is the only time prior to the Incarnation of Jesus that we find the Lord sharing a common meal with someone. Here is an un-hurried meal, shared with a friend. It's knowing who it is that shares this meal with Abraham that leaves us amazed at the sheer generos-ity of God, giving his time to his servant. Here's a day on which God came to dinner. Against the larger picture of Abraham's life, this meal had a deeper significance. We talked before about the covenant. The covenantal meal was a way of celebrating the bargain that had been made between two parties. So here is God coming personally to cel-ebrate this great covenant arrangement that he has made with Abraham.

Here is the Lord sharing this meal with his servant. He accepts the hospitality of this man as an expression of his commitment to keep his covenant with him. The leisureliness of the meal, the sheer invest-ment of time and the sharing of confidences with Abraham are all marks of friendship. I think of Jesus' words to his disciples on the night on which he was betrayed, when he tells them that he had longed to eat the Passover with his disciples before his arrest; or his promise of that day when he will eat with his people at table, with Abraham and Isaac and Jacob, in the Kingdom of God.

This idea of sharing a meal with the Lord is built into the big pic-ture of the Bible and is that one day we will sit at table at that mar-riage supper of the Lamb when Jesus returns. Behind all of those pictures is the offer of us being caught up into the friendship of God by his grace. God wants to be your closest, truest, dearest and near-est friend. And when you have him as your friend, you have a won-derful group of friends, a team of friends at your disposal, there to help and protect you: the Trinity, the triune God that we worship.

Why is the Lord come? One reason, apparently, is to shore up Sarah's faith: the Lord had appeared to reaffirm the covenant he'd made with Abraham, and now he comes to them as a couple, to include Sarah in the unfolding drama of his purpose. He's dealing with her as an individual, with her disbelief. The Lord knows that she's listening (v9). 'They said to him "Where is Sarah your wife?" And he said, "She is in the tent." The Lord said, "I will surely return to you about this time next year, and Sarah your wife will have a son." And Sarah was listening.'

In her defence, it was a tent. It was this announcement which made Abraham realise that he was talking to the Lord. Maybe he had a premonition that these visitors were supernatural early on. We're speculating, and we're not allowed to do that with the Bible, but at this point he knew for sure and the reason is that they used her new name. 'Sarah your wife shall have a son.' By the announcement of that name, and the fact that they repeat almost word for word the announcement about the birth of the son, he knew that it must be the Lord.

This time the Lord was appearing to him in the form of a stranger. That's an important feature in the Bible. The Lord is a stranger to us: there is about the Lord that which is different. Even the resurrected Lord Jesus in his risen humanity: there's something different. He appears to them as a stranger. Can you imagine the Lord turning up to dinner?

At this point, Moses reminds us (v11) that there was a problem to this promise that God has given. Abraham and Sarah are old, Sarah is barren, now post-menopausal: she is doubly dead as far as child-bearing is concerned. So (v12) 'Sarah laughed to herself, saying: "After I am worn out, and my lord is old, shall I have pleasure?"' She is thinking to herself: 'Some hope! I'm tired, and I'm past it.' And her laughter, silent in itself, is the cynical laughter of unbelief. John Stott puts it like this: 'Unbelief is not a misfortune to be pitied, it is a sin to be deplored. Its sinfulness lies in the fact that it contradicts the word of the one true God, and thus attributes falsehood to him.' But God knows what you think even when you don't say it out loud.

So the Lord (v13) says to Abraham, 'Why did Sarah laugh?' Can you imagine how embarrassed she was? 'She shall indeed bear a child.' God knew exactly what was in her mind. Sarah had heard

Hagar's testimony that the Lord knew where she was when she was far from home. Now Sarah learns that not only does God know where she is, God knows what she's thinking. There is nothing that you can hide from him: he is omniscient, he knows everything as well as sees everything.

She's also challenged to admit there's nothing too hard for the Lord. Miraculous birth and miraculous resurrection are nothing to him. To believe in such things is entirely rational: if there is a God then a miracle is not a miracle to him. It's only a miracle in our eyes. Two thousand years after Sarah, there was another girl who had no prospects of motherhood for different reasons: she was a virgin. And yet she gets a similar message from an angel that she's going to be pregnant as a result of a miracle. Mary didn't laugh but she did ask: 'How can this be since I am a virgin?' And the angel replies to her the words that echo the words to Sarah, and says 'For there is nothing impossible with God.' That language links these two events: Isaac who begins it all, Jesus who ends it all. At the beginning and end there are these miraculous births that mark out this great plan of salvation.

Sarah denies it (v15): 'I did not laugh.' For she is afraid that she's gone against God, so she starts to argue with God. God's rebuke is a reassuring sign. The God who can read your thoughts can open the womb. In fact, God's going to have the last laugh, because their son, when he's born, is going to be called Isaac, which means 'laughter'. God is more gracious with us than we deserve, and his words to Sarah are designed to build up her faith. They're gentle words, spoken to a struggling believer.

God the righteous and good (vs 16–33)

The God who is faithful and true is righteous and good. He who brings hope and life to Abraham and Sarah has come to bring judgement and death to the people of Sodom and Gomorrah. Here Abraham is identified as a prophet to whom is given foreknowledge of God's plans and judgements (v16): 'The men set out from there and they looked down towards Sodom. And Abraham went with them to set them on their way. The LORD said: "Shall I hide from Abraham what I am about to do?"'

The Lord's visit highlights the close relationship between them. It's also setting us up to understand Abraham's role as a prophet. We've seen Abraham act as a king and a priest, now he's going to act as a prophet. In his lifetime, he fulfils each of those three roles, and our Lord Jesus, his great successor, is going to fulfil those three roles perfectly. Here Abraham is being set up to be a prophet when the Lord says, 'Shall I hide from him what I am about to do?' Amos 3:7 explains it: 'Surely the Sovereign LORD does nothing without revealing his plan to his servants the prophets.' That was why in the Old Testament, the measure of a real prophet of God was: did what they say come true?

The passion that God has when he's looking at Sodom and Gomorrah is a passion for his own righteousness, and that his people – Abraham and his offspring – should understand something of the righteousness and justice of God. God wants us to know that he takes sin seriously. He will judge sin, and he deals righteously with people. From this point on, Abraham and his offspring are going to be able to point to these cities and tell their children: when you see those cities destroyed under the fiery flood of God's judgement, that is where societies eventually end when God gives them up to do what is in their hearts to do.

Verse 20: 'The outcry against Sodom and Gomorrah is great and their sin is very grave.' God takes sin seriously, and this word 'outcry' is used in a variety of ways in the Hebrew Bible. It's used of the cries of the brutalised, the oppressed, the widows and the orphans. It's used of the attacked, the victimised and the depraved. Here in Sodom there was all of that but it was the sexual sins in particular that pushed the envelope of behaviour beyond what is God-honouring.

There was an occasion when Dr Billy Graham said, 'If God doesn't judge America' (and for America let's read the whole of the Western world) 'then he'll have to apologise to Sodom and Gomorrah.' We live in a violent world. Sin offends our righteous God. It is obnoxious to him. Many things in the world don't offend us because we have become inoculated by them. Every now and then something happens that really annoys or upsets us, but by and large the things that offend God don't offend us.

God is righteous and God is good, because he doesn't rush to judgement, and so from verse 22 onward we find Abraham interceding for Sodom. Abraham is not trying to extract from God something God is unwilling to give. It's God who initiates the whole thing. By telling Abraham what he's going to do, he's inviting Abraham's involvement in this business. 'Then Abraham drew near and said, "Will you indeed sweep away the righteous with the wicked?"' The knowledge of God's certain judgement of the world should ignite in the heart of a believer a burden for the lost. That's what's happening in Abraham's heart. He's taking the place of the covenant mediator, the representative who stands between the people and the Lord, who pleads to the Lord for those who are under the condemnation of God's righteous judgement. Verse 25: 'Far be it from you to do such a thing, to put the righteous to death with the wicked, so that the righteous fare as the wicked! Far be that from you! Shall not the Judge of all the earth do what is just?'

Abraham had good motives. He had to learn though that sometimes, in earthly judgements, the righteous are caught up with the unrighteous in the unfolding of those judgements. But he is absolutely right that in the end the righteous are spared the awful judgement of hell. Notice he pleads the character of God, what God is. In the New Testament, his great successor Jesus pleads his own authority, his own standing before God, and he intercedes with God. Abraham rests on the character of God. He rests his case in God's righteousness, and that's all we can do. The reality is I do not see sin the way God sees it. My nice, middle class neighbours, there in the heart of London, are good people. But they offend the holy God. When I look in the mirror in the morning I see someone who by nature, choice and behaviour offends the holy God in ways that I cannot even begin to understand.

God the just and merciful (Gen. 19:1)

Abraham pleads, 'If you find even ten righteous people, will you not spare the city?' God says 'Yes, I will.' Then he goes back to his tent and, in justice, God judges sin.

God of justice

The opening of chapter 19 is a ferociously evil description. The two angels came to Sodom in the evening. Lot was sitting at the gate. Like his uncle, Lot saw them, got up and bowed down with his face to the earth, and he said 'Please come to my house, spend the night and wash your feet. You may rise up early and go on your way'. These are virtually the same words as those used by Abraham. They said: 'No, we're quite happy to spend the night in the town square.' Lot said: 'Please, don't do that, you've no idea where you are. Come into my house.' He made them a feast. 'But before they lay down, the men of the city, the men of Sodom, both young and old, all the people to the last man, surrounded the house. And they called to Lot, "Where are the men who came to you tonight? Bring them out to us, that we may know them"' (Gen. 19:4,5). That is, gang-rape them. 'Lot went out to the men at the entrance, shut the door after him, and said, "I beg you, my brothers, do not act so wickedly"' (vs 6,7).

He acted out of the kind of responsibility that you would expect from someone who took the hospitality of the area seriously. But notice what he went on to say (v8): 'Behold, I have two daughters who have not known any man. Let me bring them out to you, and do to them as you please.' Can you imagine any father saying that?

What we have in chapter 19:1-14 are the reasons why Sodom couldn't continue to exist. When the Lord Jesus wants to paint a picture of the dreadful end of the world, he refers us to Noah's flood and Lot's Sodom. There's a warning also in this passage for any community that despises the gospel of Jesus Christ. Here's what Jesus says in Matthew 10: 'And if anyone will not receive you or listen to your words, shake off the dust from your feet when you leave that house or town. Truly, I say to you' – here's a message for Western Europe that has abandoned the gospel – 'it will be more bearable on the day of judgment for the land of Sodom and Gomorrah than for that town' (Mt.10:14,15).

God of mercy

Lot escapes the judgement of Sodom and it's all down to mercy. His salvation doesn't depend on his righteousness. He is righteous because he believes, he's in a right relationship with God in spite of himself, and the universal principle of the way God deals with us is that we are dealt with in mercy. Lot is referred to as a righteous man (2 Pet. 2:6–9). It's incredible that Lot is called a righteous man three times. Lot is one of those people who are saved as by fire: no works to show, stripped bare of anything in which he had a good positive impact. It's all gone: saved as by fire.

You can see how much Sodom had got into Lot (v18): 'And Lot said to them, "Oh, no, my lords . . . I cannot escape to the hills, lest the disaster overtake me and I die. Behold, this city is near enough to flee to, and it is a little one. Let me escape there."' He can't throw off what he's got in Sodom, he is so tied to that place. The Lord is good to him (v21): in grace, God gives him what he asks and he is sent to that little city for a while.

When the judgement falls, Mrs Lot becomes a sodium chloride monument to the foolishness of letting the world get into your heart. We need to ask ourselves how much of the world has got into our hearts. We need to get away from the fundamentalist taboos of smoking, drinking, dancing and going to the movies, and focus on the real sins that are affecting our society: materialism; pleasure-seeking; indiscriminate enjoyment of salacious, violent entertainment; immodesty of dress; voyeurism; sexual laxity and divorce. We have allowed the world to creep into our hearts.

It gets worse

Every day Lot's righteous spirit was vexed by the things he saw, but apparently he never did anything: never raised a question or made a criticism. When eventually the men surround his house and he tries to get them to behave, they laugh at him. And the world has so got into his family that, after they escape from Sodom, his two daughters come up with this plan: they'll get their father drunk, then they'll sleep with him. One bears Moab, the father of the Moabites. And the other bears Ben Ammi, the father of the Ammonites. Sin has got into the family and is going to spread through those two tribes. All is not lost: God is able to retrieve even our sin. One of the little Moabitesses in the future, Ruth, is going to become a forerunner of the Lord Jesus, the Messiah.

Let's see the big picture. Why does God deliver Lot from Sodom? Verse 29: 'he remembered Abraham, and sent Lot out of the midst of the people.' We need to take sin and hell and judgement more seriously. Let's be intercessors for the lost.

3 Looking for a city: Genesis 20 – 24

Introduction

As we've been going through these chapters of the Bible, the search has been on for a seed. From Genesis 3:15, the promise of a Saviour-seed, a Man-child who would be born and would reverse the effects of Adam's disobedience, has been launched out into the world. We've been looking for the one who would fulfil that promise.

Was it Adam? Adam failed us. Was it Cain? No. It seems as if, in these early chapters of Genesis, we've been going through the list. Was it Enoch perhaps, this preacher of righteousness that comes in the midst of a whole catalogue of people who made no impression upon the world? It wasn't Enoch. Was it Noah, this saviour, the one who was saved through the judgement as it fell at the Flood? Noah does what God has called him to do, but he fails at the end, he is a sinner. Noah was not the offspring for whom we look.

The search for this seed drives the narrative in the whole story of Abraham. It has been hanging over us since we started these studies, and when we get to chapter 20, it's still hanging over us. The promise has not yet been fulfilled: it hasn't yet come to pass, what God is going to do. Twenty-five years have passed, the promise seems to be further away than ever. Abraham's now heading towards his century, and still there is no promise fulfilled.

Stumbling into sin

As we come to chapter 20, remember what's just happened: God has acted in judgement against Sodom and the righteous in Sodom have been saved by the intercession of this great Abraham. Abraham's been doing well for a while, in terms of living out the faith that he obviously has in the promise of God. He's got a record now of success. He fought the battles of the Lord, he kept the word of the Lord, he has taken the back seat in terms of the property issue with Lot, he's interceded for Lot, he's seen God working in remarkable ways. Get to chapter 20 and you find him stumbling into sin.

'Abraham journeyed toward the territory of the Negeb and lived between Kadesh and Shur; and he sojourned in Gerar. And Abraham said of Sarah his wife, "She is my sister"' (Gen. 20:1,2). If you've been following the story so far you'll know this is a rerun of something that happens right at the beginning of the story, in chapter 12. He goes to Egypt because there's a famine in the land, and says to Sarah, or to Sarai as she was called then, 'If anybody asks you, tell them you're my sister.' Here he is at the end of his career, after twenty-five years of living by faith in the promises of God, and he repeats the same old sin.

I want to say to all of us who've been going along the Christian journey for a little while: never get complacent. Never think that simply because you no longer have the energy of youth that you've got beyond the level of temptation, at any stage in your Christian life.

Here is Abraham plunging back into the very same sin that he was committing at the beginning. Abraham is the covenant partner of God and, though he is faithless, God remains faithful. Last year when we were studying Galatians, Steve Brady quoted Martin Luther:

'*Simul justus et peccator.*' Basically, it means simultaneously justified and sinful. That's the way a believer is. We have to be more realistic about our behaviour in our Christian lives and recognise that we will find within ourselves both of these things: a right relationship with God and an area of our lives that is not all that it should be

Abraham had been declared right with God but he's not perfect. Why do you think the Lord Jesus taught his disciples to pray every day 'forgive us our sins'? Because we need daily forgiveness. When I went to Duke Street, I introduced a prayer of confession of sin into our corporate worship, one that we say together. People were saying: why should Christians be confessing our sins? Because Jesus told us to.

Here is Abraham, the man of faith, and he's faithless. That's the issue. He asks his wife to say that she's his sister. 'And Abimelech king of Gerar sent and took Sarah.' And God intervenes. 'But God came to Abimelech in a dream by night and said to him, "Behold, you are a dead man because of the woman whom you have taken, for she is a man's wife."'

Abraham is putting the whole programme of redemption at risk. Abimelech could have had him killed for what he was doing. That would have been it, because God's purpose was that it would be the offspring of Abraham and Sarah who would be the forerunner of the Saviour of the world. So he's putting Sarah, himself and Abimelech at risk. Whenever the Church sins, it puts the world at risk, and it's a shameful thing when it happens.

He is rebuked by a pagan king and his witness is ruined

It's very interesting that Abimelech realised that this was wrong. Abimelech understood on the basis not of special revelation or a written scripture, but on the basis of his own conscience, informed by God's general revelation to all humanity, that adultery was wrong. He recognises this, and challenges Abraham. God has warned him (v7): 'Now then, return the man's wife, for he is a prophet, so that he will pray for you, and you shall live.' This is the first time in the Bible that the word 'prophet' is used.

Abraham says 'There's no fear of God in this place.' He was wrong, because this pagan king, though he was never a believer, had a fear of God. Abraham was the one who didn't have a sufficient fear of God. What you have here is an illustration of the Church failing the world. We manifest by our behaviour, or by our lack of behaviour, a blatant disregard for the word, the law, the life and the authority of God over us. There are times when things happen in the world as a result of the disobedience of the Church. Martin Luther, commenting on the Muslim invasion of Europe, when the Turks were at the gates of Vienna, said: 'Islam is the rod of God against a disobedient Church.' In every age society brings upon itself the judgement of God and sometimes the judgement of God is a result of the Church not being the Church. That's the case here. And the solution still lies with the Church, as it does here (v17): 'Then Abraham prayed to God, and God healed Abimelech.'

The solution still lies with the disobedient Church. In spite of all our imperfection, rebellion and abuse of our office and position in society, the solution to society's ill still lies with God's people. Remember Jonah? Jonah's the only one who's asleep. Very often the Church, which is asleep in its indifference, needs to be awakened by the power of God, to accept its responsibility, to plead with God for the nation and the world, as Abraham here pleads for Abimelech. Martin Luther said that the face of the Church is the face of a sinner. And we need to be aware of that and challenge ourselves. Judgement begins in the house of God.

Proving the promise (Gen. 21)

Abraham has been waiting for this moment for twenty-five years. It was promised when he was in Mesopotamia, repeated when he moved to Canaan, reinforced several years later, and then reinforced again several years after that. Now he's a hundred years of age. And then it happened (v1): 'The LORD visited Sarah.' Here's the word of God fulfilled in action, God performing this miracle in the womb of this woman. It's a miracle! Here it is at long last!

What do you get in the text of the Bible? Well, 'the LORD did to Sarah as he had promised. And Sarah conceived and bore Abraham a son in his old age at the time of which God had spoken to him' (Gen. 21:1,2). And that's it. Is this what we waited for? Why the understatement? Part of it is to say: he's here, but *he's* not here. The offspring's arrived, but *the* offspring hasn't arrived. The promised one has arrived, but the Promised One, the Messiah, hasn't come. In fact, if you look at the life of Isaac, his is an almost inconsequential life, with one major high point.

The issue of election

The miracle happens, and Sarah's ninety plus, and she's laughing. God's word has been fulfilled, the miracle has occurred, and the rest of chapter 21 is to deal with another issue which is often a hard issue for us. I think we have to say that, although it's something that some of us want to affirm it as strongly as we can, nonetheless it's always hard to get our heads around the issue of election, and the fact that there's an election of grace. God is going to work his purposes out through Isaac and not through Ishmael.

Ishmael is as defiant as his mother and they mock the arrival of God's miraculous gift. The word for laughter occurs in this section several times: five times in the birth of Isaac, and then the same word in a different shape occurs in the second half of this chapter. This time it's the laughter of mockery. Ishmael is not mentioned at all here: he is referred to only as the son of Hagar. Although he is treasured by God, nonetheless, the focus is going to be on Isaac because he is the child of promise. Isaac is the fulfilment of what the Lord had promised.

Looking at the bigger picture of the Bible, the promise given to Abraham, that culminates in the arrival of Jesus, begins with a miraculous birth and ends with a miraculous birth in the Bible. That's some amazing bracketing together. It begins and ends with God visiting his people. And it begins and ends in a wider context of enmity, hostility. You would expect that perhaps Ishmael might be glad to have a little brother arrive on the scene but he's hostile. That rings true in terms of what happens when the Lord Jesus arrives in the world. He comes to his own people and his own people have no time for him. Paul, in Galatians 4, allegorises the story of Hagar and Ishmael like this

> For it is written that Abraham had two sons, one by a slave woman and one by a free woman. But the son of the slave was born according to the flesh, while the son of the free woman was born through promise. Now this may be interpreted allegorically: these women are two covenants. One is from Mount Sinai, bearing children for slavery; she is Hagar. Now Hagar is Mount Sinai in Arabia; she corresponds to the present Jerusalem, for she is in slavery with her children (Gal. 4:22-25).

Paul is saying you can allegorise this story. Hagar and Ishmael felt in comparison to the blessing of Isaac, who was in the line of promise, that although they were in the house, they didn't really belong there. Paul is saying that somebody who lives their life according to works, there's always resentment involved in everything that you do. Maybe you're relating to God on the basis of performance and not promise. You're living by law and not by grace. Paul says 'you, brothers, like Isaac, are children of promise' (Gal. 4:28). You know you belong. If you've been saved by the grace of God and are delighting in the grace of God that he's shown to you in Christ Jesus, then you should know that you belong in the family. Isaac certainly knew he belonged. And there are these two kinds of people. One lives by performance, who has no affection for the Lord Jesus Christ. But if you know that you are a child adopted into the family of God, the liberation comes, because you love the Son. That's the picture that Paul paints: we have to decide where we are.

In the New Testament, in James 2, it says

> Was not Abraham our father justified by works when he offered up his son Isaac on the altar? You see that faith was active along with his works, and faith was completed by his works; and the Scripture was fulfilled that says, "Abraham believed God, and it was counted to him as righteousness" – and he was called a friend of God. You see that a person is justified by works and not by faith alone (James 2:21–24).

People read that and they think 'Ah! You say by works and not by faith alone.' But what James is talking about is this incident here in chapter 22. Where does it say that Abraham was justified by faith? Back in chapter 15. He's already justified by faith, he's already in a right relationship with God, but his justifying faith is justified by the works that flow from it. In other words, the faith, which alone saves, is never alone. Our faith is the only instrument of our justification. When I believe in the Lord Jesus, at that moment I am declared right with God. And God gives me his Holy Spirit, and as the Holy Spirit begins to work in my life, things begin to change.

In chapter 22 we see the evidence of the change in Abraham, and it's the biggest test Abraham's ever going to face (v1): 'After these things God tested Abraham and said to him, "Abraham!" And he said, "Here am I."'

Here the word 'tested' relates not to Isaac, but to Abraham, because the real danger was not to the child, but to the man of faith. Abraham is torn between his faith in the divine promises and the command of God to nullify those promises, between his affection for God's gift and his affection for God.

I want you to follow this very closely. God said "'Take your son, your only son Isaac, whom you love, and go to the land of Moriah, and offer him there as a burnt offering"'(Gen. 22:2). There's something that's often missed in Bible translations: it's unprecedented in divine commands anywhere in the Bible. Literally, the Hebrew could be translated '*please* take.' I think it's the only place in the Bible where God says to any human being 'please.' It flows from Abraham's readiness to respond to God. And there's one word that's repeated over and over again in this section that heightens the tension, and it's the word 'son' (vs 2,3,6,7,8,9,11,12,13,16). It's being rubbed in, the catastrophic implications of what God is telling this man to do. He is to go with his son to Moriah, the site of the later Temple in Jerusalem, and he is to sacrifice him. Now that's a very difficult thing for us to deal with. It raises all kinds of questions.

There's something else not to miss: the relationship between Abraham and Isaac. Why do you think God's doing that? It's because this is a relationship that God the Father understands perfectly well.

To this severe test there is prompt obedience (v3), 'So Abraham rose early in the morning, saddled his donkey, and took two of his young men with him, and his son Isaac.' It's all action. It takes them three days to get there, often when something significant is going to happen it takes three days to prepare for it, just as it took three days to prepare for the resurrection of Jesus. 'Then Abraham said to his young men, "Stay here with the donkey; I and the boy will go over there and worship and come again to you."' I think he took the servants so that they would be eyewitnesses to the event that was going on. Their presence also stresses the isolation of Abraham as he does this great thing. He must leave everything behind to do the will of God. Notice Abraham's faith in action here (v5): 'I and the boy will come back to you.' Now the New Testament actually identifies that Abraham so believed the promise of God that he worked out that God could raise the dead. Here's how it's put in Hebrews 11: 'By faith Abraham, when he was tested, offered up Isaac, and he who had received the promises was in the act of offering up his only son, of whom it was said, "Through Isaac shall your offspring be named." He considered that God was able even to raise him from the dead, from which, figuratively speaking, he did receive him back' (Heb. 11:17-19).

The narrative takes us further. Twice we're told the father and the son 'went together' (vs 6,8). Isaac carries the wood for his own destruction, just as two thousand years later another would carry the wood for his own destruction, up the same hill, to be crucified outside the city wall. And as they're going Isaac (v7) says to Abraham his father, 'My father, behold the fire and the wood, where is the lamb for the burnt offering?' Just as in another drama another was to wait for soldiers to come and arrest him, and as he agonised in prayer to his Father, he submitted trustingly to the Father's will.

What does Abraham say (v8)? 'Abraham said "God will provide for himself the lamb for a burnt offering, my son." So they both of them went together.' This is the point of the Abraham story, the high water mark not only of Abraham's faith but of God's revelation. At this point the whole story slows down. As they reach the place, build the altar together, father and son, lay the wood in order on the altar, as the lad stands while he is bound by his father and then laid on the wood on the altar, and as the father lifts his knife and the son remains without struggling on the altar: there is cooperation between the father and the son. Can you imagine it?

This is the picture God gives us to help us understand something of what is going on in the future when the Lord Jesus is going to the cross. There is absolutely no biblical evidence at all or basis for suggesting that the Lord Jesus did something that extracted something from the Father that the Father was unwilling to give, or that somehow or other the Father was angry at his Son. As the Lord Jesus Christ on the cross was made sin for us with our sin, his Father loved him at that moment, loved him in his humanity. Even as his wrath was being poured out against us on the Person of his Son, as he who knew no sin was made sin with our sin, the Father loved his Son.

The knife is about to fall, the throat is about to be cut and, at that moment, 'Abraham lifted up his eyes and looked, and behold, behind him was a ram, caught in a thicket by his horns.' Abraham didn't hesitate: he took the ram and offered it up as a burnt offering instead of his son. The language here is incredible, 'Behold.' This is where the English Standard Version helps us because it uses the same word throughout whenever it's translating. The NIV's a very good Bible for reading because it finds different words to say the same thing, so it sounds more interesting. The ESV is more accurate in that it translates, as much as possible, one word for one word. Where do you hear this word behold again in the Bible? What does John the Baptist say twice in John 1? He says 'Behold! Behold, the Lamb of God, who takes away the sin of the world.'

These Jews in the desert, as they're listening to Moses teach this, would think of Passover, when the angel of death came. The firstborn son in every home in Egypt was going to die except where people took God's word seriously and killed the lamb, which spared them from the judgement. They would understand that this was a propitiatory sacrifice, this burnt offering. And look at the name: Abraham called the place, 'The Lord will provide.'

The promise of the lamb stands. It stands, until the Lamb of God appears in the world. And God does not spare his only Son. No wonder Jesus said, 'Your father Abraham rejoiced that he would see my day, he saw it and was glad.' The day he saw that ram die on the altar, in place of Isaac, Abraham had a pre-figuration of the cross, and he was glad.

Claiming the land (Gen. 23 – 25)

The last days of Abraham start with the wife of his youth dying. Sarah died. Abraham has believed the promise of God, so he gets into a bit of real estate; he buys a burial site, just a little place to bury his family in Hebron. Sarah's bones are buried in Hebron, and it becomes the resting place of the patriarchs, a silent witness to the promise of God. Why? Because Abraham and the patriarchs are looking for a city that has foundations, whose Builder and Maker is God. Abraham remarries, he has more children, and then, at a hundred and seventy-five, he pops his clogs and is gathered to his people.

He is not simply placed beside Sarah's bones; rather he is caught up into the living fellowship of the redeemed; just as we shall one day all sit down with Abraham, Isaac and Jacob and all of the redeemed at that heavenly banquet in the Kingdom of God. Now what do we look for? We follow Abraham in his faith; we are Abraham's offspring, because we believe like Abraham, the father of the faithful. We look for the fulfilment of the promise of the land, that's all that's left. We believe not only in the life everlasting but in the resurrection of the dead, that in the flesh we shall see God. As we come to the end of this week we, like Abraham, having faith in the same promises of God, also look forward to that city whose Builder and Maker is God.

Abraham and Isaac

by Richard Hasnip

The sun was hot, the ground burnt black, as they staggered up
the hill
To honour God Abraham had sworn an oath to kill
Isaac his son. He closed his eyes and wiped the sweat away
Isaac stopped in front of him, he turned to him to say

'Father we have flint for fire, rope and razor blade
But where's the animal to sacrifice? I feel afraid
I fear to see you look at me, I fear to see your knife
God forbid you've brought me to this place to take my life.'

Abraham looked on his son with anguish in his eyes
The tears were running down his face as he whispered this reply

'Oh Isaac lad my dearest boy, my dearest darling son
God has claimed your life again, claims you beloved one
I cannot refuse his will, him I must obey
In heaven you will sleep tonight, you'll see God's face today.'

'Dad I'll never fight with you, I'll suffer for God's will
Take my life and open up my throat upon this hill
Do it quickly please, don't wait; my fear is rising fast
Spill my blood and end my life and let me breath my last.'
The sun was hot the ground burnt black as Abraham obeyed
Almighty God and crying loudly, raised the razor blade
But God's own voice called out to him before the boy's blood wet
the land
And Isaac's eyes they opened wide to see what stayed his father's
hand.

'My servant stop I don't require that you should take this life
You'll find caught by his head in thorns a better sacrifice.'

And Abraham freed his son with tears and killed instead
A ram caught in a thicket, stunned by what the Lord had said.
He staggered home with Isaac back towards his loving mum
So God spared Man the very thing that He himself has done,

For like that ram in thicket caught, God's own Son He would slay
With thorns crowning his gory head to take our sins away.
The sun was hot the ground burnt black upon the barren hill
As God watched soldiers lead his Son to Calvary to kill.

Colossians
by Charles Price

Charles Price

Charles Price is the Senior Pastor of The People's Church in Toronto, Ontario, Canada, with a weekly congregation of 3500 people. He has a weekly hour-long television programme, Living Truth, which is broadcast coast to coast in Canada each week, as well as in the United Kingdom, Europe, India, Australia, New Zealand and Indonesia. His Sunday messages are also translated into Farsi and broadcast each Tuesday night into Iran, Iraq and Afghanistan. He has preached in over fifty countries on five continents, and is the author of seven books, some of which have been translated into other languages. He has been married to Hilary since 1980, and they have three children: Hannah, Laura and Matthew.

1 The supremacy and sufficiency of Christ: Colossians 1:1–23

Introduction

There were things going wrong in the Church in Colosse: serious misunderstandings over what the context and substance of the Christian life is. Whether they were aware of it or not, I don't know. The subtlety of error is usually that we drift just a little bit away from the truth and don't recognise it to be error and then a little bit more and before very long, we're up to our necks in error. Paul doesn't describe what all the errors are but we know by his emphases. In chapter 1 the supreme theme is the supremacy of Christ and that is always the cornerstone of any deviation from truth: we lose the position of Christ. In chapter 2, the big issue is the sufficiency of Christ. Not only is Christ supreme but he himself is our strength. His involvement in our lives is the means by which we're equipped to live the life that he's called us to live. Once you lose the centrality and the sufficiency of Christ, you have to replace him with something: legalism, religious observances, where the focus moves from internal life and internal intimacy with God to external patterns of behaviour imposed by rules. We can easily romanticise the Early Church, but when you read the epistles of Paul, you find in nearly all of them that believers have become drawn away from the key fundamental issues of the Christian life.

Background to Colossians

This letter is called the letter to the Colossians, not because Paul is writing to some very big people but because they live in a town called Colosse. Colosse is in today's Turkey, and it seems that Paul had never been there himself but on his third missionary journey, he came to Ephesus. He stayed there for three years and saw phenomenal success in Ephesus, and from that epicentre, people went out with the gospel, until the whole province of Asia had become evangelised. It doesn't mean converted but they'd been exposed to the gospel of Jesus Christ. It's very likely that one of the men converted in Ephesus was a native of Colosse, Epaphras, and he went back to Colosse and preached the gospel to them. In Colossians 1:7, Paul says, 'You learned it [the gospel] from Epaphras, our dear fellow servant, who is a faithful minister of Christ on our behalf'. Later, in chapter 4, Paul refers to Epaphras as 'one of you', ie, he lives in Colosse.

This morning I want to talk about three things that Paul talks about: what he says about himself; what he says about his readers in Colosse and what he says about his message

Paul on himself

His opening statement is: 'Paul, an apostle of Christ Jesus by the will of God'. This is a typical way to open a letter in Paul's day. You put your name first. And he describes himself as an apostle of Jesus Christ. What does it mean to be an apostle? The word 'apostle' literally means to be a 'sent person'. Paul is saying 'I am a man under orders. I'm not doing my own thing.' That raises the question, an apostle of whom? And he tells us: 'an apostle of Jesus Christ'. 'In other words' says Paul, 'amongst you my task is very simple: it's to represent Jesus Christ: his interests, his message, to the extent that what you see and hear from me will be utterly consistent with what you would see and hear from Jesus Christ.' That is a very important thing for those of us who are preachers of the gospel; we have no message of our own or if we do, it's corrupt.

Why is Paul an apostle? He tells us: 'by the will of God'. It wasn't that Paul was looking for a career in Christian ministry; Paul was a man with a divine call from heaven. That is the best way to live on Earth, with a sense that my work here has been determined from heaven. How did Paul know that? Because God told him and the Church told him. Those two are important to understand together. God told him when he was first converted to Christ. In Acts 9:15, it says 'the Lord said to Ananias, "...This man is my chosen instrument to carry my name before the Gentiles and their kings and before the people of Israel."'

Right from the day he was converted, Paul knew 'God has set me apart for a particular purpose.' But Paul was very wise: he didn't begin his apostolic ministry until the Church heard the same message, approximately twelve to fourteen years later. In Acts 13 it says, 'In the church at Antioch there were prophets and teachers ...While they were worshipping the Lord and fasting, the Holy Spirit said, "Set apart for me Barnabas and Saul for the work to which I have called them." So after they had fasted and prayed, they placed their hands on them and sent them off.'

Notice two very important things: the Holy Spirit said to the Church, 'I called him. You send him.' There are to be no lone rangers in Christian ministry. I often meet people who believe God has called them to something in particular but nobody else seems to recognise it and they usually complain. It may be that they are part of a church that is not sensitive to the Spirit of God and for those of us in leadership, that must be one of the most important things we do, asking the Lord, 'Who is it in this church that you're preparing for particular areas of Christian ministry?' But when God calls a person, you can be sure that those who are spiritually sensitive will, in the course of time, recognise it. Together with the call and equipping of God is the sending of the Church. That is the pattern in Acts 13. The will of God is not designed to be a very individualistic thing that we discern and hope other people will understand: it is something that is discerned corporately.

Paul on his readers (vs 2–14)

He addresses them (v2) as 'To the holy and faithful brothers in Christ at Colosse'. I want to pick out three things here in three tenses:

Past tense

'We always thank God, the Father of our Lord Jesus Christ, when we pray for you, because we have heard [past tense] of your faith in Christ Jesus and of the love you have for all the saints'. 'You folk have a reputation' he says, 'that you have faith in Jesus Christ and you love people.' When he says 'We've heard of your faith in Jesus Christ', it does not mean they have got their doctrine sorted out. What he is saying is, 'There are things about your life that can only be explained in terms of Jesus Christ being active amongst you.'

That's what faith in Jesus Christ does. Faith, by definition, is an attitude of dependence on an object that allows the object on which you depend to do something for you. You're exercising faith right now in the chair on which you are sitting, and that means that the chair is doing something for you, not that you are doing something for the chair.

Paul says, 'We have heard that there are things going on in Colosse, where the only explanation is that Jesus Christ is doing something.' That has to be the explanation of our lives, if they're spiritually authentic. The measure of our authenticity with God is not that we're doing all kinds of things for God but that there are things God is doing in and through us that are inexplicable, apart from the fact that God is doing them. Then Paul goes on to say, 'you have love for all the saints.' You can't detach those two: dependence on Jesus Christ always leads to loving others, because that's what Jesus Christ does and, when we depend on him, we take on his characteristics.

Present tense (v9)

Paul goes on to say, 'For this reason, since the day we heard about you, we have not stopped praying for you and asking God to fill you with the knowledge of his will through all spiritual wisdom and understanding.' I recommend praying the prayers of Paul. They are never for the superficial, they are always for the fundamental things. He's saying here, 'I am praying that you will be filled with the knowledge of God's will through spiritual wisdom and understanding.' That is in direct contrast with the statement in Colossians 2:8, where he says, 'See to it that no one takes you captive through hollow and deceptive philosophy, which depends on human tradition and the basic principles of this world rather than on Christ.' In other words, 'These traditions that you've adopted are ones which any man in the street will understand, because they are purely human in their reasoning and logic. I'm praying there will be things about you and the way you go about life that will be inexplicable to the man on the street because they derive not from human wisdom but from the Spirit of God.'

The big temptation always is to humanise our Christian lives, to reduce what we do to some neat strategic plan that is completely predictable, rather than living in that relationship with God where the knowledge of his will comes through spiritual wisdom.

Future tense (vs 10–12)

Paul goes on to say

> And we pray this in order that you may live a life worthy of the Lord and may please him in every way: bearing fruit in every good work, growing in the knowledge of God, being strengthened in all power according to his glorious might so that you may have great endurance and patience, and joyfully giving thanks to the Father, who has qualified you to share in the inheritance of the saints in the kingdom of light.

This is a fantastic prayer and, if you look at it very carefully, you'll see a recurring theme: it's all about God. It's about living a life worthy of the Lord, pleasing him, bearing fruit, growing in the knowledge of God's strength and so on. Some people say, 'That is impractical. Give me some practical stuff.' I have many conversations with people in this area. I might say to them, 'Have you asked God about this?' They often look at me blankly and say, 'I don't know how to do that, that's why I am coming to talk to you.' I say, 'Come and talk to me when you've first talked to God.'

The Christian life can only be lived when we recognise that it is supernatural: it derives from the presence and activity of God himself within us. This is the subtlety of what was going on in Colosse, they were replacing God with patterns, rules and regulations, which made everybody totally predictable.

Paul on his message (vs 15–18)

This is one of the great Christological passages of the New Testament. It is vital that we have a true view of Jesus Christ. Later in chapter 1:28, Paul says, 'We proclaim him, admonishing and teaching everyone with all wisdom, so that we may present everyone perfect in Christ.'

The deity of Christ

'He is the image of the invisible God, the firstborn over all creation. For by him all things were created: things in heaven and on earth, visible and invisible, whether thrones or powers or rulers or authorities; all things were created by him and for him. He is before all things, and in him all things hold together.'

'Creation' Paul says 'is by him and for him and held together by him.' There's nothing left out of this: things in heaven, things on Earth, things that are visible, things that are invisible, throne, powers, rulers, authorities; whether good or bad, hostile or not, they're all created by God. Not only that, but what he has brought into being, he maintains in being. And he is affirming here that Jesus Christ is completely equal with the Father and the Holy Spirit. That is a fundamental doctrine of the New Testament.

Now a Jehovah's Witness may well tell you, on the basis of these verses, that Jesus Christ is not equal with his Father, because (v15) he's described as the firstborn over all creation. Mormon doctrine teaches that God created Christ and then Christ created the universe. But the biblical use of this term 'firstborn' is not usually about birth order but about birth right. To be firstborn is about being heir of all that belongs to the father. Therefore this is not about the creation of Christ, but about his pre-eminence in the whole of creation. Not only that, (v18) he's the firstborn among the dead. Not first chronologically: but he's the firstborn from among the dead in the sense that his resurrection is the one that has priority and our resurrection depends upon his.

The humanity of Christ

You might read this and say 'I see a lot about his deity here but not much about his humanity.' Look in verse 15: 'he is the image of the invisible God.' Does that description ring a bell? That is exactly the description given of Adam in Genesis 1:26. Human beings, as God intended them to be, were to be a visible physical expression of what God is like and therefore, when it says of Jesus, 'he is the image of the invisible God' it's not talking about his deity but about his humanity.

This is very important. Scripture tells us no one has ever seen God and we are forbidden, in the Ten Commandments, to construct an image of God of any kind. There is only one visible and physical way in which God intended to portray himself, and it was in humanity. There are things which are true of God, of course, which are not true of human beings. God is all-powerful: we are not. God is all places at all times: we do not share his image in that sense. God is omniscient, he knows everything there is to know, and we don't. God is immutable, he does not change: we do. Therefore, when it describes human beings as being created in his image, it is in his moral image. God is love, we're intended to be loving; God is kind, we're intended to be kind. It's his moral character that he was to display in human beings. So if we saw the way Adam treated Eve, we would have seen what God was like. If we saw the way Eve treated Adam, we would have seen what God is like. God's intention was that human beings would be the visible physical expression of his own nature, but something went wrong. The day that Adam ate, he died spiritually. He became, in the words of Paul in Ephesians 4, 'separated from the life of God' and he no longer showed what God was like.

Now Jesus Christ has come onto the scene. Paul describes him in 1 Corinthians as the 'last Adam, the second man': the second man as God intended man to be. Jesus Christ is the image of the invisible God. Any image or understanding of God that is not fleshed out in the Person of Jesus Christ is faulty. If you want to know what a real man is supposed to be like, look at Jesus Christ.

With increasing frequency these days, new things come into the Church of Jesus Christ, some of them bizarre, and people are often confused. Let me suggest to you one important criterion. We ask the question, of whatever the incident is, 'Is it true of Jesus?' If it is true of Jesus, it is the truth; if it is not true of Jesus, it may not of itself be intrinsically wrong but it's not truth, so don't encourage it and don't preach it.

The goal of the gospel, says Paul in Colossians 3:10, is to 'have put on the new self, which is being renewed in knowledge in the image of its Creator.' In other words, you are being made what Adam was created to be, in the image of the Creator. As Paul told the Corinthians, this is an ongoing, lifelong process. The measure of our spiritual growth is, 'Is there more evidence of Jesus Christ in our characters than there was last year?' Which means the way I, as a husband, treat my wife more quickly reminds me of Jesus than it used to. The way we spend our money; the way we talk to the neighbours; the way we talk about the neighbours when they are not listening: all these express the character and the image of God. That is what spiritual growth is. We grow from one degree of glory to another, into his likeness.

An elderly man said this: 'God has revealed himself in three Testaments: he's given us the Old Testament, the New Testament and there is the You Testament. Which one do you think your neighbours are reading? They're reading the You Testament and that will either tell them the New Testament has something to say or that the New Testament has nothing to say.' We take a long look at Jesus, because the measure to which he is the image of the invisible God, that image is to be expressed in us. All that God is inhabits all that Christ is, and here's the utter fantastic truth of the gospel, which we'll talk about tomorrow: all that Christ is inhabits all that you are.

The Lordship of Christ (v18)

This image of the Church as the Body of Christ is one that Paul uses often. He doesn't say 'The Church is *like* the Body of Christ', he says 'The Church *is* the Body of Christ.' What does it mean for Christ to be the head of the Body, the Church? Does it mean that he founded it and is the head in the sense that he's the source, he started it all off? Or does it mean he's the head as in he is the monarch over it, as the Queen is the head of this country? The problem is Queen Elizabeth reigns but she doesn't rule. Is that the position of Jesus Christ: he's a sort of monarch of his Church? We operate in his name? Or does it mean that he is in charge of the Church, he has opinions about it, he has an agenda for it? Of course, that is the explanation. My head is indispensable to the function of my body, it is where the nerve centre is, it is where I think. My body functions as it connects to the head.

I was at a pastors' conference and someone spoke on the theme, 'What would Jesus have wanted for his Church?' I was very disappointed with this message. He asked 'What would Jesus have wanted if he was still here?' He is still here! It's not 'What *would* he have wanted?' but 'What does he want?' It's present tense: he's active. That's why the Church of Jesus Christ must function, first and foremost, in relation to him, not in relation to our own plans. The task of Church leadership is to discern the mind and the will of God. We have to be discerning and there are ways in which we can discern the mind and will of God.

We are the members of that Body and the Holy Spirit is the life of that Body and we operate, first and foremost, in dependence on him and in interdependence upon one another. 'And this' says Paul to the Colossians 'is where you are losing the substance of the gospel. You've introduced human logic, human reasoning, philosophies that are based on the principles of this world to make you totally acceptable to the man in the street, because everything you do is totally predictable and logical.' But when you are living in union with Jesus Christ, the folks in the street are going to scratch their heads and not understand what is going on, because it is a spiritual, supernatural enterprise where Jesus Christ himself is the head, the model of true humanity. 'And' says Paul, 'you've lost his deity, you're in danger of losing his humanity and you're losing his Lordship and, if you lose that, you will end up with a hollow religious enterprise. It will be spiritually dead.' It is the activity of Jesus himself in the Christian, and therefore in the Church, that makes the Church of Jesus Christ what it is.

2 The mystery that unlocks Christian living: Colossians 1:24 – 2:5

Introduction

The word 'servant' is probably a demeaning word or at least it has that connotation, and not many of us would describe ourselves as servants. But actually the word carries great dignity and Paul often refers to himself as being a servant, normally of Jesus Christ. Many of the opening statements of his epistles describe him that way but here in Colossians 1 he describes himself as a servant in two other ways. In verse 23, he describes himself as a 'servant of the gospel' and then in verse 24, he describes the Church as being the Body of Christ and says (v25): 'I have become its servant.' The pattern here is that to be a servant of Jesus Christ is to be a servant of the Church, and then to be a servant of the gospel, to present the word of God in its fullness. Paul talks about the word of God coming to a place of fullness: not in the sense of volume, but of completion. And this is something that he describes here as a mystery (v25).

Cracking a mystery

If you and I are going to understand the gospel in its fullness, we've got to crack a mystery. 'It's a mystery' says Paul, 'that has been hidden for generations.' When Abraham received the covenant that God made with him, he scratched his head and said, 'Something's missing. What is this all about?' When Moses received the Law, all the instructions about the priesthood and the blood sacrifices, he scratched his head and said, 'I've understood exactly what God has said to me but what in the world is all this about? There's something missing.' When Jeremiah preached his heart out, he went back home, sat down, usually wept and said, 'There's a missing ingredient, a mystery.'

The idea of mystery, as Paul uses it, is that there's something that's been covered over, a missing piece. God's revelation is progressive. We don't have everything in the books of Moses and God revealed his truth through thousands of years of history. But the nature of the progress is not from half truths to whole truths: the nature of the progress is from promise to fulfilment. There are teasers all the way from Genesis right on through the Bible, teasers that are promises that are fulfilled ultimately when this mystery becomes known. If we are going to understand what Scripture is, the revelation of truth that God has given to us, we will find it is actually best read backwards. We've heard what the mystery is, let's go back. You see it all the way through the Old Testament, which is why the Old Testament is not just a background to the New Testament. It is full of spiritual truth that finds its culmination in the revelation of this mystery which Paul talks about here (v27): 'To them God has chosen to make known among the Gentiles the glorious riches of this mystery' [the means by which everything else in the Christian life will make sense and it's seven words]: 'Christ in you, the hope of glory.'

I'm going to talk about that this morning because if this is the mystery that's been hidden for ages, it is vital that we understand it. This is the word of God coming to its fullness, says Paul. It's about four things: a Person (Christ); a place (in you); a purpose (the hope of glory) and appropriation.

A Person

The first word in understanding this mystery is Christ. Later, in chapter 2:2-3, Paul says, 'My purpose is that they may be encouraged in heart and united in love, so that they may have the full riches of complete understanding, in order that they may know the mystery of God, namely, Christ, in whom are hidden all the treasures of wisdom and knowledge.' If this word of God comes to its fullness in Christ, which is the context here, we need to ask, what is the word of God? Scripture speaks of this in two ways. There is the written word of God, the Scriptures, inspired by the Holy Spirit. It's authoritative. We believe the word of God not because of what it says but because of who it is that's saying it: God. John opens his Gospel (Jn. 1:1) by writing, 'In the beginning was the Word, and the Word was with God, and the Word was God.' The Word – *logos* – is Christ himself.

Christ is the Word and Scripture is the word of God and there's a difference between them. The difference is: Scripture is true but it is not the truth; Christ is the truth. 'I am the truth' he said. Let me explain what I mean by that. If you ever get hold of an aeroplane timetable, you might discover that there is an aircraft that leaves London's Heathrow airport on Saturday at one o'clock, and arrives in the city of Toronto at four o'clock local time on the same day. That would be true, at least I hope it is, because I plan to be on that flight on Saturday. But, although the timetable is true, it is true only in the sense that it bears witness to the truth which is the aeroplane. The timetable won't get me to Toronto, it'll tell me how to get there, by bearing witness to the truth which is the aircraft.

Scripture is true, but one day Jesus criticised some Jews (Jn. 5:39): 'You diligently study the Scriptures because you think that by them you possess eternal life. These are the Scriptures that testify about me, yet you refuse to come to me to have life.' 'You think the Scripture *in itself* is the truth. It isn't, it is true but the truth to which it bears witness is me.' We must never detach what is true from the truth. The mystery is not a doctrine or a theology. This mystery, first and foremost, is a Person: Christ. Detach the truth from what is true and the Scripture becomes a dead book.

This Word of God in its fullness is not word as in words, it is the Word as embodied in Christ who is the truth, the revelation, the image of the invisible God. That's why he says, 'that you may know the mystery of God.' What is it? Namely, Christ: in whom are hidden all the treasures of wisdom and knowledge. That is what comes out of Christ; all the wisdom and knowledge that you need. That's why those of us whose task it is to preach have one message to preach: it's Christ. There are a million ways to preach Christ but of every sermon I preach, I ask the fundamental question: 'What am I saying about Christ?' So if you're not talking about Christ, you're not preaching. Unless the truth we proclaim needs Jesus Christ to make it work, it's not the gospel.

A place

On the day of Pentecost, Christ came to inhabit his own people. That's why Luke, writing Acts, begins it by saying, 'In my former book, Theophilus, I wrote about all that Jesus began to do and to teach.' Now the implication of that is Luke's Gospel is all that Jesus began. But the whole story's in Luke! Yet he says, 'That's just what Jesus *began* to do.' Volume 2 is what Jesus continued to teach, the same Jesus but in a new Body, which is why the Church is his Body. It's the same Jesus, it's just a different means of doing his work. Jesus said to his disciples in John 14:17, just before his crucifixion, about the Holy Spirit, 'He lives with you and will be *in* you.' That's the difference Pentecost is going to make: he will be *in* you. Previously the Holy Spirit was *with* people and *for* people but he's going to be *in* people and that, of course, is what makes a person a Christian.

Paul said in 2 Corinthians 13:5, 'Examine *yourselves* to see whether you are in the faith; test yourselves.' What would you test? Not your Bible or your theology: he says 'Examine yourselves.' Do you not realise that unless Jesus Christ is in you, you will fail the test?

When I was Principal of Capernwray Bible School, 180 or so students would come every year. Often on the first Sunday of the term in September, I would preach on this verse. I'd say 'I want to start with an examination. Here's the examination; is Jesus Christ in you?' And these were students who'd come to a Bible school. It was remarkable how often someone would come to me and say 'I don't think I'm a Christian.' I'd say, 'It would be a good idea to become one, then you'll enjoy the Bible school much more.' The symptoms are very straightforward. When you have life, you know you have life because you have appetite, a hunger and thirst for righteousness, a hunger and thirst to know God, a hunger to be like Christ.

This means so much to me because in the first few years of my Christian life, I didn't understand this. I became a Christian at the age of twelve and I thought that when I became a Christian, God gave me three things: a ticket, a certificate and a catalogue. The ticket said, 'One way to heaven' – I knew I was going to go to heaven when I died. The certificate said, 'This is to certify that Charles Price has had all his sins forgiven: signed God.' I knew I was forgiven. And God had given me what I saw as a catalogue, the Bible. The Bible told me all kinds of good things that I could get from God: God had some sort of spiritual supermarket with all these goodies and an errand boy called the Holy Spirit. My job was to read the catalogue, find out what I could get from God, put in my request – which was called praying – and the Holy Spirit would send me whatever it was I'd ordered. So, for an example, I read the Bible and found out I could have some love. 'Lord, would you please give me some love?' I imagined the Holy Spirit coming with a tube of love. And that would wear off. I'd read the catalogue, I'd have some joy. Then that would wear off. I'd read the catalogue, I could have some peace. I'd read the catalogue, I could have power. It always wore off.

I came to a point of despairing, wondering whether the Christian life would ever work and then I discovered that when I became a Christian, God gave me only one thing: himself. The new birth is the imparting of the Spirit of God, the life of Jesus Christ in me. As Colossian 2:2 says, we 'may know the mystery of God, namely, Christ, in whom are hidden all the treasures of wisdom and knowledge.' Love is a fruit of the Spirit, joy is a fruit of the Spirit; peace, power are all consequences of the life of the Spirit of God within us.

I knew Romans 6:23: 'For the wages of sin is death, but the gift of God is eternal life in Christ Jesus our Lord.' I thought that verse meant that eternal life was something God gave me, but actually that isn't what it says. It says the gift of God is God. There's only one eternal life. The word 'eternal' is different to the word 'everlasting'. 'Eternal' means to have no beginning and no end; 'everlasting' means to have no end but presupposes a beginning. There's only one eternal life with no beginning and no end, the life of God. The day I became a Christian, God himself came to live within me and this becomes the strength.

Let me illustrate this, if I may, from D.L. Moody. Moody would pick up a glove in front of his congregation and say, 'This glove was made in the form and the image of a hand.' And he'd say to the glove, 'Glove, you were created in the image of a hand, I'm going to put you down on this side of this pulpit. I have over here a book. You were created in the form and the image of a hand, so would you please demonstrate your ability to behave like a hand, and pick up the book?' Nothing would happen. Moody would say, 'Glove, I'm talking to you: pick up the book.' Nothing would happen. He would dance around and nothing would happen. He'd say, 'How is this glove ever going to pick up this book? There's only one way.' Moody would put his hand into the glove, reach over and pick up the book. What's happened to the hand? What's happened to the glove? The glove has become inhabited by the hand and all the power of the hand has become the power of the glove. Moody's point was that this is what it means to be a Christian.

Every illustration has its shortcomings and we're not passive pieces of material. Nevertheless the principle is true that the ability that we have to live the life that God has called us to live is not by doing it for Jesus but by living in such intimacy with him, dependence on him and obedience to him, that he is the source of our life and strength. So much so, as Jesus said in Matthew 5:16, 'let your light shine before men, that they may see your good deeds and praise your Father in heaven.' The source of your goodness is God himself. What they actually see is God at work in you. The mark of authenticity in the Christian life is that people in our presence become conscious of

Jesus Christ. It is the life of God in the soul of man that makes the Christian life possible and exciting.

Andrew Murray was a great South African writer, who preached from this platform, probably on a different campus but in this place, in the late nineteenth century. When I was involved in jointly writing the history of the Keswick Convention, I read many of the old services to see what were they preaching back in those days. And Andrew Murray said this, 'There are two invitations that Jesus gave. If you understand these two invitations, you'll understand the Christian life. The first invitation is "Come to me; if you're weary, if you're heavy laden, if you're burdened, come to me, I'll give you rest." The second invitation is "Abide in me. Having come to me, if the source of your strength and your life is me, because you abide in me and I abide in you, and we live in union together, you will bear much fruit. Your life is going to make an impact."' Murray said, 'Understand these two things and the rest of the Christian life falls into place.' I think he was profoundly right. If we have a problem in our day, it is because we've reduced the Christian life to psychological processes, things we're supposed to do because they're Christian things to do, rather than the intimacy and union with Christ himself who is our life.

A purpose

Why does he live in us? 'Christ in you the hope of glory.' And that does not mean heaven. In Christian jargon, glory has become a word for heaven. That is not the biblical use of the word. What is our essential problem? It's sin. What is sin? The word sin means to miss the mark. If you took an arrow, shot it at a target and missed, it was called sin. If you missed by half an inch, it was called sin. If you missed by half a foot, it was called sin. If you missed by half a yard, it was called sin. If you missed by half a mile, it was called sin. If you shot in the other direction, it was called sin. Sin is not a measurement of how bad we are, it's a measurement of how good we're not, if you understand the difference. God is not particularly interested in how bad you are, God is interested in how good you're not. So you don't know what sin is unless you know what the mark is that you've missed.

What is the mark? Romans 3:23: 'for all have sinned and fall short of the glory of God.' The glory of God is the moral character of God. It is that which he displayed in the Lord Jesus Christ. John wrote in John1:14, 'The Word became flesh and made his dwelling among us. We have seen his glory, the glory of the One and Only, who came from the Father, full of grace and truth.' When he said 'We have seen his glory', what did he see? Did he see a bright light above Jesus' head? No, he's saying, 'We saw in Jesus Christ the moral character of God. We saw what God was like.' Because human beings were cre-ated to display the image, the character of God. 'Now, in Jesus, we saw the glory of God. In the way he would cross the road to sit with a dirty woman everybody else was embarrassed to be seen with, the way he would touch lepers, we saw what God was like.' This is the glory of God. But the human dilemma is this: we have sinned and come short of the glory of God, we've missed the target, we've ceased to portray what God is like. So what's the gospel about? It's Christ in you, your hope of hitting the target; it's getting back to what we were supposed to be.

The evidence of Christ in you is not that you're going some-where, though you are, but that you are displaying something of his character. Of course, it's filtered through our old nature which we're lumbered with for the whole of this life. So, as Paul said 'we are being changed from one degree of glory to another into his image.' Christ in you is your hope of hitting the target, of being what human beings were created to be; a display of the character of God. This is why holiness is not an additional add-on to the Christian life, it is the inevitable consequence of the Christian life.

Paul refers to this later in Colossians 3:3 when he says, 'When Christ, who is your life, appears, then you also will appear with him in glory.' That does not mean a place. Heaven is glorious, but that is a position. When Christ, who is our life, appears, our position will be glorified. That's the goal to which we're going: we're going to be glo-rified.

So it's Christ in us, being himself in is, that expresses his character through us. Going back to Moody's glove illustration, the explanation for what the glove does is the hand. If I were to put a hand into a glove and punch you in the face, would you blame the glove? No, you'd want to have a word with me. That's why the gospel is good news to anyone, because it's not about what you do for Jesus, it's what you, in your relationship with him, will allow Jesus to do through you.

Appropriation

Paul says (v28), 'We proclaim him, admonishing and teaching everyone with all wisdom, so that we may present everyone perfect in Christ. To this end I labour, struggling with all his energy, which so powerfully works in me.' In case you might begin to think that somehow the Christian life becomes passive, it isn't like that. He says, 'to this end, I labour.' Mine is the labour and the struggle: his is the energy. Do not for one moment think that when Christ is our life and strength, we somehow become exempt from battle. In the very next verse, Paul says 'I want you to know how much I am struggling for you and for those at Laodicea' (Col. 2:1). There's struggle, there's labour: the Christian life is characterised by that. It's a battle but I battle in his energy. We're going to get tired, disappointed and hurt: it's a battle.

We live in dependence on him and obedience to him: those two things can never be separated. Obedience and dependence are like two wings on an aeroplane. Which do you think is the most important wing? Obedience without dependence leads to legalism. Dependence without obedience would lead to unhealthy kinds of mysticism. But obedience and dependence is dynamism. For all the great characters of Scripture, when we have any detail about the way they lived or acted, those two things were fundamental in their daily experience. Obey what God says and trust who God is. Paul is saying in Colossians that it's a mystery, it's been hidden, and at last it's come to its fullness. The mystery is Christ living in you, your body being his dwelling place, your hope of hitting the target, your hope of glory, being what you were designed to be. So to this end I labour, struggling with his energy which so powerfully works in me. How's this going to work out in day-to-day living? If you want to know the answer to that, come back tomorrow morning.

3 True and false spiritual growth: Colossians 2:6–23

Introduction

Derek Tidball, in one of his books, tells of a man who visited Florida and he ordered fresh orange juice in a restaurant. Florida is the orange state, full of orange groves. This restaurant was surrounded by orange groves. The answer he got was, 'I'm sorry, we can't give you any orange juice, the machine is broken.' Surrounded by millions of oranges but no juice. Sometimes, I suspect, for many of us, the Christian life feels like that. In Colossians 2:2-3, Paul talks about treasures. Why is it, then, that so many of us feel like we live in poverty? In verse 9, he says, 'In Christ all the fullness of the Deity lives in bodily form, and you have been given fullness in Christ.' How come then so many of us feel so empty?

How do we get the juice out of the oranges? This is what Paul talks about in these verses. I'm going to call them, firstly, 'The true spiritual life' and secondly, 'Pseudo-spiritual life and growth.' By 'pseudo', I mean it purports to be real. It looks real and many folks think 'This is the real thing' but actually it is not. It is extremely subtle. Remember this is a first generation church Paul is talking to, not folks who have inherited some kind of Christian culture but never known spiritual life. They are relatively new Christians, seduced by this seemingly attractive means of getting the juice out of the orange.

True spiritual growth

'So then, just as you received Christ Jesus as Lord, continue to live in him, rooted and built up in him, strengthened in the faith as you were taught, and overflowing with thankfulness' (Col. 2:6-7). I like the rhythm of the Authorised Version: '*As* you have received Christ Jesus your Lord, *so* walk in him'. In other words, the way you receive him is the way you live in him.

How did I become a Christian?

As you received him, so live in him. You become a Christian on the basis of redemption and faith. Repentance is turning from myself, my sin and my own abilities. Faith is turning to him, to his ability, and relying on him to do in me what I cannot do in myself. Repentance says 'I can't,' faith says 'God can.' The basis on which anyone has ever become a Christian is that they come to a point of realising 'I can do absolutely nothing about my condition myself. I cannot save myself.' Repentance is acknowledging that and repentance means to change the mind. You change your mind about yourself, your sufficiency, your ability and your sin. You turn to faith, and say 'I can't, but you can.'

Paul makes that very clear (v13): 'When you were dead in your sins and the uncircumcision of your sinful nature, God made you alive with Christ.' Who did it? God did it. 'He forgave us all our sins, having cancelled the written code, with its regulations, that was against us and that stood opposed to us . . . He took it away, nailing it to the cross.' The grounds on which anybody becomes a Christian is surely the work of God. When you discover that you're utterly bankrupt, and realise *you* can't, but *God* can save you on the basis of the work of Jesus Christ, then you become a true Christian.

Now, as you receive Christ Jesus, so live in him. What's the basis of living the Christian life? Exactly the same: I can't, he can. I can no more live the Christian life in my own strength than I can become a Christian in my own strength. This is liberating, you know, because every morning when I wake up, I know this: I cannot live the Christian life today. If I thought I could, I would be a fool. But there's a Person who lives inside of me, and inside every Christian: the Lord Jesus, by his Holy Spirit. As you received him, so live.

The Lordship of Christ

Christianity is bringing your life under the Lordship of Christ. One of the themes in the early part of Colossians is the sovereignty of God. Paul said to them, 'Remember when you received Christ, you received him as Lord.' Those are the conditions on which you receive him into your life. The act of becoming a Christian involves submission to Christ as Lord and you cannot live the Christian life other than in the recognition that Jesus is Lord.

When I was a young Christian, I had the impression that there were two kinds of Christian. There was the average Christian, and there was the super-deluxe version. The average Christian knew Christ as their Saviour, and the super-deluxe version meant not just knowing Christ as Saviour but having Christ as Lord.

As you read your Scriptures, you'll find that is not so. A young man came to Jesus one day, the rich young ruler. Jesus was coming out of Jericho and this man came running up, fell on his knees and said, 'Good master, what must I do to inherit eternal life?' Jesus said, 'What about the commandments?' He said, 'All these I have kept since I was a boy.' I don't believe him, and I'm sure Jesus didn't, but that is what he said. Then Jesus said, 'One thing you lack. You're a rich man, go and sell your possessions and then come and follow me.' And it says that the man went away very sad, because he was very rich.

Why did Jesus make an issue of the man's riches? Is it because it's wrong to be rich? The Bible warns there are dangers to being rich, but it doesn't say it's wrong. But what it does say is that no one can serve two masters. What he's saying to this man is this, 'If you want to receive eternal life, understand that it involves receiving a master, and that is a problem: you've already got a master. So first get rid of your master, then come and follow me.' And the man went away empty-handed. He was not willing to trade his master for Jesus Christ.

Jesus didn't run after him and say, 'I'm sorry, I didn't mean to frighten you. Come back, let's talk about this. Let's negotiate, see what type of Christian you'd like to be. Would you like your sins forgiven? You want to go to heaven when you die? Fine. Now listen, you're a rich man, aren't you? I've got some ideas for what I'd like to do with your wealth. Would you like me to implement that? You wouldn't? Ok, don't get uptight. What I want to know is, do you want my will or yours? I'll leave that to you. Would you be willing to be filled with the Holy Spirit? What's that? As long as nothing funny happens? We'll keep it calm. Now you really want to go to heaven when you die and have your sins forgiven. You don't really want much more than that. Well, by all means become a Christian, that's great. It won't be very satisfying, but later you can always come and get rededicated, but at least welcome to the family. If you get sat on by a camel, you'll at least know where you're going.'

Is that what Jesus said to him? Of course it wasn't. I fear we say things like that today. What's the lowest common denominator? I know that God looks at the heart; I know that many of us have no clue about the Lordship of Christ when we come to know Christ as Saviour. But he looks at the heart. Is the heart saying 'I want Jesus'? Or 'I want Jesus as my servant'? Often we grow in our understanding of this. But Jesus is called Saviour 24 times in the New Testament; he's called Lord over six hundred times. Although it's wonderfully true that he saves, he saves because he comes to be who he is within us, and who he *is*, is Lord. And sometimes, to relegate Jesus just to being Saviour is to rob him of what he really wants to accomplish in our lives.

Let me illustrate this. My wife is here this morning, and we've been married 28 years. She's got lots of ability and talent and she's a lovely cook. If you were to come to our home, you'd enjoy her cooking. Suppose I brought her up on the platform, and said, 'Ladies and gentlemen, I'd like you to meet my cook.' What do you think she'd say? I'll tell you what she'd say: 'Who did you say I was?' 'I said you were my cook.' 'I'm not your cook!' 'Of course you are, you cook for me, don't you? And I bought you a cookbook and a cooker!' 'I cook for you, but I'm not your cook! I'm your wife.' The day we got married, I didn't say, 'I take you to be my personal cook.' I said, 'I take you to be my lawfully wedded wife.' When she became my wife, I got a cook, I got a gardener, I got all kinds of things. But she's not my cook.

It's wonderful that Jesus saves us. But if that's all we think in terms of, we tend to think of him as being our servant, rather than going beyond that to recognise that he is Lord. Paul says if you want to get the juice out of the orange, if you want to live this life effectively, you have to recognise that he is Lord, to whom you live in utter and complete submission. As you receive Jesus as your Lord, continue to live in him as your Lord, rooted and built up in him as your Lord.

Strengthened in the faith you were taught

You're not going to live this Christian life by osmosis; you've got to be instructed. Paul says that you are strengthened in the faith as you are taught. You need to be taught. And to submit our lives to the Lordship of Christ is to submit our lives to the word of Christ. You can't separate those. Colossians 3:16 says, 'Let the word of Christ dwell in you richly as you teach and admonish one another with all wisdom, and as you sing psalms, hymns and spiritual songs with gratitude in your hearts to God.' As we cannot live the Christian life detached from the activity of the living Christ within us, we cannot live the Christian life detached from the word of God dwelling in us richly.

And how is this done? As far as I can see, the primary reason in the New Testament for coming together is to be taught and instructed. The reason you sing songs is not to make God feel good about himself but because, through them, we are teaching one another the things of God. That's why we are so grateful for people like Keith and Kristyn Getty and Stuart Townend, because they're writing hymns full of truth. Many times in my own experience, it's a song that reminds me of God's goodness and faithfulness.

Thankfulness

Thankfulness is a key theme of the New Testament. In Colossians 3:17, Paul says 'And whatever you do, whether in word or deed, do it all in the name of the Lord Jesus, giving thanks to God the Father through him.' Whatever you do, he says, do it in this spirit of giving thanks. Now why is this so important? Because thankfulness is acknowledgment of dependence on someone. That's why thankfulness is such a key ingredient in the Christian life, because it's acknowledging 'God, thank you, we trust you.'

The language of faith is not 'Please', the language of faith is 'Thank you.' If you read the prayers of Jesus, he never says please, but he constantly gave thanks. When he fed the loaves and fish to the five thousand people, it says 'when he'd given thanks . . .' He was saying, 'Father, thank you, this is your situation not mine. I trust you.' At the grave of Lazarus, he said, 'Father I thank you that you hear me.' This spirit of thankfulness permeates the New Testament.

How do we get the juice out of the orange? Recognise this: as I receive him, so I live in him. On the basis of my own bankruptcy I turn, I trust him, I live under his Lordship, I bring myself under the instruction of the word of God and I live in a spirit of thankfulness. That's the nature of true spiritual life and growth.

The pseudo-spiritual life

Paul is writing this because in Colosse there is a pseudo-spiritual life and growth going on, that purports to be the real thing, and it is especially subtle. It is the danger that the Church of Jesus Christ is constantly living with.

Idle spiritual notions

Verse 18: 'Do not let anyone who delights in false humility and the worship of angels disqualify you for the prize. Such a person goes into great detail about what he has seen, and his unspiritual mind puffs him up with idle notions.' There are some exotic spiritual experiences that people are talking about here, but Paul calls them 'idle notions' and 'unspiritual', which is very interesting because they sound super-spiritual. He explains the cause (v19): 'He has lost connection with the Head, from whom the whole body, supported and held together by its ligaments and sinews, grows as God causes it to grow.' Colossians 1 speaks of Christ being the head of the Body, his

Church. What has happened here is that there are folks within the Body who have actually lost connection with the Head, meaning instead of living out of his strength and direction, they're on their own. They're living a Christian life that has its root in themselves, in their own discipline and ability. What happens then is that you replace the internal spiritual life, that God imparts to us, by external rules and regulations – some biblical, some traditional – by which we measure our spiritual progress. We all need some means of regulating our behaviour, some marks by which we might measure that we are getting somewhere, that encourage us to keep on track. But when it ceases to be your relationship with Jesus Christ, and the intimacy that needs to characterise genuine spiritual life, it becomes instead not a life that works from the inside out – the Spirit of God in us expressing himself through us: it works from the outside in. So I follow the regulations in the hope that somehow this external behaviour will make for spiritual life within me and this leads to two things that Paul addresses here: legalism and judgmentalism.

Legalism

> Since you died with Christ to the basic principles of this world, why, as though you still belonged to it, do you submit to its rules: "Do not handle! Do not taste! Do not touch!"? These are all destined to perish with use, because they are based on human commands and teachings. Such regulations indeed have an appearance of wisdom, with their self-imposed worship, their false humility and their harsh treatment of the body, but they lack any value in restraining sensual indulgence (Col. 2:20–23).

In other words, he says, you make rules for yourselves – 'Don't handle, don't taste, don't touch' – but these rules don't come from life, they are externally imposed. The word legalism, which I've already used, can be thrown around carelessly and it's not a word in the New Testament as such, but the issue of legalism is present right through the New Testament. I want to show you why legalism looks good, but is evil. Legalism is a means of treating biblical truths about behaviour as regulations to be kept in our own strength. We believe that, in keeping them, we will earn or stay in God's favour. Legalism is present when we do the right things, and therefore the legalist is almost always a moral person, that's why he finds it difficult to see that there's something wrong with it. But it works from the outside in. It doesn't change us, it just house-trains us.

We have a couple of cats at home, we got them when they were kittens, and when they came to live in our home, we taught them that there are certain things we don't do in our house. And if you came to our home, you'd be very impressed with the good behaviour of our cats. But if we leave the house in a hurry in the morning and maybe some frozen meat is left out on the counter to thaw, when we come back there might be tooth-marks in the meat. Because although the cats behave perfectly when we're around, they have no moral conscience about what they're doing.

All the law can ever do is house-train us. There are lots of Christians who have been thoroughly evangelically house-trained. You know who they are, because when they're home behind closed doors, they behave differently. They're not driven by the life of Jesus Christ in them; they're driven by the rules. Paul says, 'You folks in Colosse are falling into this legalism where you say, now you're a Christian, you've got to behave in a certain way.'

The law that God gave in the Old Testament has a very interesting career in the Scriptures. When God gave the law to Moses, the whole nation was asked, 'Will you obey all the words of this law?' They said, with good conscience, 'We will.' They didn't but that's what they said. Joshua reaffirmed the covenant. The law is a revelation of the character of God, and God's character is what we were created to express when we were made in his image. So the law is the external description of what God's character is like and against it you discover, as the Israelites discovered very quickly, failure.

Jesus came to bring the new covenant and it is described in Jeremiah 33 in this way: '"This is the covenant I will make with the house of Israel after that time," declares the LORD. "I will put my law in their minds and write it on their hearts. I will be their God, and they will be my people."' So he says, 'I'm going to relocate the law from tablets of stone to the human heart.' And he told Ezekiel (Ezek.

36:27): 'And I will put my Spirit in you and move you to follow my decrees and be careful to keep my laws.' The Spirit of God within us is totally consistent with the law of God, but the law of God only works from the outside in. All it can ever do is house-train us. The very same requirements of the law are now written within our hearts by the Spirit of God (who never lies, never steals, never commits adultery and is never greedy) as he, in us, expresses the law of God through us and our behaviour. The end result is that we behave utterly consistently with the law. And pseudo-spiritual growth is saying 'Forget about the word of God, forget about living with the intimacy of God, just be evangelically religious and keep the rules. It's a lot easier.'

Judgmentalism

Paul talks about that in verse 16, 'Therefore do not let anyone judge you by what you eat or drink, or with regard to a religious festival, a New Moon celebration or a Sabbath day.' The general point is that once we start making rules by which we measure our own Christian life, we inevitably become judgemental of everyone else who does not live by the same rules, and we seek to impose those rules.

Every generation has its own culture, of course. Every Christian church seems to have its own culture. A friend of mine was in Holland talking with some Christians about the worldliness of American Christians, and these Dutch Christians were complaining about the way American Christians dress – this was some years ago – the fact that they all wear make-up and go to the movies. He said, 'They were so upset, their tears were trickling down their cheeks along their cigars and dropping into their beer.' Whereas in America, they're probably lamenting the worldliness of the Dutch Christians who smoke cigars and drink beer.

Have any rule you want in your own life, for your own benefit, but please don't impose them on anybody else, and don't judge people by them. If you have to judge people at all, do it by the fruit of the Spirit. When you lose connection with the Head, instead of jettisoning your Christianity, which you probably won't do, you simply prop it up with rules, and become very critical of those who don't keep them. Paul says in verse 20, 'Since you died with Christ to the basic principles of this world, why, as though you still belonged to it, do you submit to its rules "Do not handle! Do not taste! Do not touch!"?' Paul is saying this is actually worldliness. Worldliness is not necessarily running out and doing lots of wild things. Worldliness can be living by the law.

I'm often asked, 'What is the Christian position on such and such?' I sometimes reply, 'What if there isn't one? What if you need to do the hard work of talking to God about this yourself?' So, how do you get the juice out of the orange? How do you live it? Realising, as you received him, so live. I can't, he can. So I depend on him, I surrender every day to him as Lord, I am taught from his word, I live in that spirit of thanksgiving and I don't try to live by law. I let the life of God be the source of how I live. I don't judge others. It challenges me that churches like the church in Colosse hadn't been around for three generations before the whole thing got tired. This is a first generation church, making the easiest mistake to make, to turn from looking to Christ to looking to the rules and laws. It makes us worldly, living according to the basic principles of this world, rather than living in Christ.

The crucified God: Isaiah 52 and 53

by Peter Maiden

Peter Maiden

Peter Maiden is Keswick Ministries' current Chairman, and also the International Director of Operation Mobilisation. He travels extensively to fulfil his commitments with OM, which has staff in 112 countries. Peter serves on the board of a number of other Christian groups, is an Elder of Hebron Evangelical Church in Carlisle, and an honorary Canon of Carlisle Cathedral. He has written two books, including *Discipleship*, the first in the Keswick Foundation series. Peter enjoys family life with his wife, Win, and their three grown-up children and seven grandchildren.

The Crucified God: Isaiah 52 and 53

The crucified God:
Isaiah 52 and 53

Introduction

This week we're concentrating a great deal of our attention on the Creator God and only yesterday you were looking at Isaiah 40. There are some amazing statements in that chapter. Let me remind you of a couple of them (v21)

> Do you not know? Have you not heard? Has it not been told you from the beginning? Have you not understood since the earth was founded? He sits enthroned above the circle of the earth, and its people are like grasshoppers. He stretches out the heavens like a canopy, and spreads them out like a tent to live in. He brings princes to naught and reduces the rulers of this world to nothing. No sooner are they planted, no sooner are they sown, no sooner do they take root in the ground, than he blows on them and they wither, and a whirlwind sweeps them away like chaff.

And then the twelfth verse of Isaiah 40: 'Who has measured the waters in the hollow of his hand, or with the breadth of his hand marked off the heavens? Who has held the dust of the earth in a basket, or weighed the mountains on the scales and the hills in a balance?'

God is so great that he needs this whole universe as a tent to live in and, in comparison with him and with his greatness, we humans, even the most powerful of us, are like grasshoppers. Kings and princes take their seats of power and seem so secure and permanent in those seats but no sooner are they sitting in those seats of power than God removes them. That's God revealed to us in Isaiah 40, so what is this we're reading in Isaiah 52 and 53? Someone so disfigured and so marred, despised, rejected and crushed and yet, as we read more carefully, in the middle of this weakness, this man of sorrows was raised, lifted up, highly exalted and sprinkling (another translation would be startling) many nations.

Who is this passage referring to?

A number of scholars have proposed that the Servant here is the nation of Israel, appointed as God's agent in relation to the nations, but I think it's quite clear that the Servant is unmistakably not a nation but an individual. He is an individual who will supremely fulfil the mission that God gave to the nation of Israel, through his own innocent suffering. When you look into the New Testament, we see this passage being applied to the Lord Jesus on a number of occasions. Jesus applies the passage to himself more than once (Lk. 22:37): he's speaking to his disciples, just before his arrest, and says: 'It is written: "And he was numbered with the transgressors"; and I tell you that this must be fulfilled in me.'

Groom argues that Paul, in Romans 4, 2 Corinthians 5 and in 1 Corinthians 15, has Isaiah 53 in his mind as he presents the death of our Lord Jesus Christ. So there is little doubt that Isaiah 53 refers to a Person, an individual Servant and that Person is our Lord Jesus Christ.

What is happening here?

To understand this, I think we have to look at the context. The man who divided up our Bible into chapters did a magnificent job but he was only a man and his chapter divisions are not inspired. I think everyone is agreed he made a slight error because from chapter 52:13 right through to the end of chapter 53 is the fourth of the Servant Songs of Isaiah, which begin in chapter 42. At the beginning of the Song, the Lord introduces his Servant to us. What was the task of this Servant? To discover that, you have to go back to chapter 49:6, where, in the first Servant Song, God says the ministry of the Servant is to bring blessing to a remnant in Israel, light to the Gentiles and salvation to the ends of the Earth.

We're reminded here of the great covenant promise of Genesis 12, and those first three verses, where God says to Abraham, 'I will make you into a great nation and I will bless you; I will make your name great, and you will be a blessing. I will bless those who bless you, and whoever curses you I will curse; and all peoples on earth will be blessed through you.' There is this extraordinarily gracious promise of God, out of the chaos, out of the sin of those first eleven chapters of Genesis. He will not bring worldwide destruction, as you might imagine, but global blessing which will touch every nation on Earth. Here again in Isaiah, through his Servant, the Lord is promising blessing: firstly, to a disobedient nation, or at least to a remnant within that nation, and he's promising to be a light to the ends of the Earth. If you look at the next two chapters in Isaiah, especially if you've got a New International Version, you'll see from the chapter headings that this Servant accomplishes this two-fold task: the heading of chapter 54 is 'The future glory of Zion' and that of 55 is 'Invitation to the thirsty.' There this blessing goes way beyond the remnant within Israel (v1): 'Come, all you who are thirsty, come to the waters; and you who have no money, come, buy and eat! Come, buy wine and milk without money and without cost.'

How is he going to achieve this task?

As you read through the Servant Songs, it becomes increasingly clear that this cannot be accomplished without suffering. So, in the second Song, we read (Isa. 49:7), 'This is what the LORD says – the

Redeemer and Holy One of Israel – to him who was despised and abhorred by the nation . . ."' And then, in the third Song, there's a very specific detailed prophecy of the coming sufferings (Isa. 50:6): 'I offered my back to those who beat me, my cheeks to those who pulled out my beard; I did not hide my face from mocking and spitting.' But it's in this fourth Song that this coming suffering is expanded upon.

The Song begins, as we've seen, with the Lord introducing his Servant, and I think it is important to take in this fact. The Second Person of the blessed holy Trinity has agreed to be his Father's Servant and he's agreed to be our Servant. That should cause our hearts to respond in thanksgiving and worship. Immediately there's the assurance that this Servant is going to act wisely (or that he will 'prosper': the Hebrew can be translated either way). We're told where this wise service will lead. He will be raised, lifted up, highly exalted. So his wise service will ultimately lead to the triumph of his Resurrection, Ascension and exaltation. It's so important to appreciate that that was always the eternal plan: an exalted victorious Christ who perfectly served his Father and accomplished complete salvation for us. The cross was no failure. As Peter speaks to the crowd on the day of Pentecost, he makes this very clear: 'This man was handed over to you by God's purpose and foreknowledge.' But this exaltation will not come before complete humiliation.

Alec Motyer, in his magnificent commentary on Isaiah, asks the question, 'Why did no one recognise the truth about the Servant?' And he has three answers. Number one: his apparent earthly origin, pointing to a human family tree. The people of his day said, 'Is this not the carpenter's son? He's just a normal human being.' Secondly, he grew up before the Lord, so how can he be the arm of the Lord if he's a distinct person? Thirdly, there was no evidence of any distinctiveness. The Servant was not noticeably well built, impressive or handsome: it was not easy at all to believe that he could be the Lord who had come to save. But then finally, of course, to see him on a cross, his appearance so disfigured beyond that of any man: this could not be the Messiah.

Note the words in verses 4 and 5: 'stricken, smitten, afflicted, pierced, crushed, punishment, wounds' – hardly what the population expected in the Messiah but amazingly, Isaiah says, 'the arm of the Lord is being revealed.' Right here in the midst of this crushing, the arm of the Lord is being revealed. This phrase 'the arm of the Lord' points to his power. So what action is our Lord taking, as he extends his arm at this moment? The Servant is described as 'a man of sorrows' but they were not his own sorrows (v4): 'Surely he took up our infirmities and carried our sorrows'. This is the language of substitution. 'He took up our infirmities' – the word means to lift up off someone. The word 'carried' means to shoulder, to take your burden as his own. But verse 5 goes dramatically further; if verse 4 is the language of substitution, then verse 5 is undoubtedly the language of penal substitution: 'But he was pierced for our transgressions, he was crushed for our iniquities...' He has punished the Servant for my iniquities, for my sin and shame. He has punished Jesus for what Jesus shouldered for me.

Again I think we need to pause and ask whether we're enjoying the fruit of what Christ has done for us. Yet so many Christians still carry what Christ has taken from us. I think of a lady who never comes to the Communion service in my home church without worrying whether she should be there. There's one particular issue in her life and doctrinally, she knows she's forgiven but she wonders whether Jesus really could have shouldered what she did. She's certainly a believer, with a genuine deep love for the Lord Jesus but Satan, for thirty years, has robbed her of the joy and the peace which Jesus went to the cross to provide for her. I don't know about your past life, I only know about mine, but there is nothing in your past life that Jesus, if you're a believer, did not take from you.

Never forget the truth of the scapegoat. In Leviticus 16, God is instructing Moses how Aaron is to approach him. When he comes into the most holy place, he's to enter with a young bull for a sin offering and a ram for a burnt offering and then, from the Israelite community, he's to take two male goats for a sin offering and a ram for a burnt offering. Aaron has to offer the bull for his own sin to make atonement for himself and his household and then he has to cast lots for the two goats – one lot for the Lord and the other for the scapegoat. And the goat whose lot fell to the Lord had to be sacrificed for a sin offering.

Then with the scapegoat: 'He is to lay both hands on the head of the live goat and confess over it all the wickedness and rebellion of the Israelites – all their sins – and put them on the goat's head. He shall send the goat away into the desert in the care of a man appointed for the task. The goat will carry on itself all their sins to a solitary place; and the man shall release it in the desert' (Lev. 16:21–22).

They had a preacher at Willow Creek in Chicago, some years ago now, who brought a live goat on the stage with him as he preached on this passage. At some point, they ushered the goat off the stage and out of the building and as it went out of the building, he shouted, 'The goat has left the building!' and there was a huge cry from the audience, about sixteen thousand people, because this image had hit them, that all their sins were shouldered by our scapegoat, the Lord Jesus.

Listen to Matthew 8:14:17

> When Jesus came into Peter's house, he saw Peter's mother-in-law lying in bed with a fever. He touched her hand and the fever left her, and she got up and began to wait on him. When evening came, many who were demon-possessed were brought to him, and he drove out the spirits with a word and healed all the sick. This was to fulfil what was spoken through the prophet Isaiah: "He took up our infirmities and carried our diseases."

Motyer comments on that account: 'The Servant took upon himself everything that blights our lives.' I almost feel like stopping there: the Servant took upon himself everything that blights our lives. Of course, we don't see in its completeness today. Diseases still affect us. The guilt of our sin has been completely dealt with but sometimes the consequences of those sins continue to blight our lives. But John, by revelation, has seen the future and this future is all because of the work of Christ. What did he see? God himself, with his people, wiping away every tear from their eyes. 'There's no more death, mourning, crying or pain for the old order of things has passed away.' So in the middle of our sorrows and failures, we can look back to the cross where the Lord Jesus shouldered everything and God forever dealt with it. Then we look forward to this reality when even the remaining consequences of those sins and sorrows will be dealt with by God who will personally wipe away every tear from our eyes.

In verse 7, we're given a further crucial insight into the work of the Servant. If you keep up to date with Christian theology in the Western world, you'll know that there's considerable confusion at present over penal substitution. I believe this can be traced back to a failure to emphasise, very often, the truth of this verse. Some people reject the penal element in substitution because the image they have is of an angry father punishing a victim. But here in verse 7 a critical truth is underlined: the knowing submission by the Servant to the Father's will. The Servant offers no resistance as these events unfold. He doesn't even argue against it. He doesn't open his mouth in opposition. He was the willing, consenting, obedient substitute. So if you ever get involved in this controversy about penal substitution, never allow in your mind any image of an angry father punishing an unwilling or ignorant victim. The whole of the Trinity was working in harmony for our salvation.

What are the results?

Go back to the quite remarkable beginning of the Song (Isa. 52:14) which speaks of the Servant being disfigured to a dreadful degree, beyond that of any man. But then, to our astonishment, we're not brought to the end of a sad story. Instead we read (v15), 'so will he sprinkle' – or startle – 'many nations. Kings will shut their mouths because of him'. Or, as the NIV margin puts it, 'so will many nations marvel at him'.

You can see a similar change of emphasis in chapter 53:10. In the first half of the verse, the Lord has crushed his Servant, making his life a guilt offering but then we read 'he will see his offspring, he will prolong his days and the will of the Lord will prosper in his hands.' As one commentator puts it, 'He who was crushed under the will of the Lord, now lives as the executor of that will.'

Motyer, in his commentary, encourages us to compare the death of the Servant with the death of the powerful and earlier in Isaiah 14, there is a description of the death of the powerful:

The grave below is all astir to meet you at your coming; it rouses the spirits of the departed to greet you – all those who were leaders in the world; it makes them rise from their thrones – all those who were kings over the nations. They will all respond, they will say to you, "You also have become weak, as we are; you have become like us." All your pomp has been brought down to the grave, along with the noise of your harps; maggots are spread out beneath you (Isa. 14:9–11).

What a contrast with the death of the Servant: 'So shall he sprinkle many nations and kings will shut their mouths because of him.' That has certainly been the case and is still increasingly the case, as the Church of Jesus Christ grows dramatically in so many nations around the world.

Living as many of us do here in the United Kingdom or in Western Europe, we don't get the true sense of what God is doing in his world today; as the death and resurrection of the Servant leads to the sprinkling of many nations. In South Korea, in 1900, there was no Protestant Church and the missionaries of those days said, 'This is a nation which it's impossible to penetrate.' Today, thirty percent of the nation of South Korea are evangelical Christians. There are seven thousand evangelical Protestant churches in the city of Seoul alone and some of them are so large, for us in Western Europe, it almost blows our circuits to think about them. I was preaching in one in Seoul just last year and the first service is at 6 o'clock in the morning and there were four thousand people in the church. At 8 o'clock, there were four thousand more, at 10 o'clock there were four thousand more, at 12 o'clock there were four thousand more and at   2 o'clock there were four thousand more. I was completely bored with my message the fifth time I preached it. Twenty thousand people just in that one church, worshipping the Lord Jesus.

Go to Indonesia, a Muslim country, and the movement to Christ from Muslims has been so huge that the government of Indonesia will not reveal the figures because they feel that Muslims will react violently – or even more violently – to the growth of the Church in what is traditionally a Muslim nation. And what about China? In

1950, the country was closed to foreign missionaries, with one million believers in the country at that time. I've read some of the prayer letters of those wonderful missionaries of 1950 and they were saddened. They said, 'We just don't know what's going to happen in China. It's probably going to lead to the death of the Church.' But what has happened? We don't really know but a conservative estimate would be that there are eighty million Christians in China in 2008.

I was in Afghanistan just some months ago and on the previous occasion I met all the missionaries in the country. Not one of them were discipling a believer from a Muslim background. Then the Taliban came in and it looked like the worst day possible for the Church of Jesus Christ in Afghanistan but, since the Taliban, Afghans have been turning to Christ as never before. Not one of our workers in Afghanistan today is doing much else than personally discipling Afghan Muslims who've come to Jesus. They say, 'Thank God for the Taliban' because Muslims saw and they said, 'If this is Islam, if Islam can present itself in this way, then that's the last thing we are interested in.' They're looking for alternatives.

If you're in the Berber area of Algeria at the present time and you want to go to church, you'd better get there early because so many Berber Muslims have come to faith that they're queuing to get into church on a Sunday. About sixty thousand Berber Muslims have come to Jesus just in the past few years. So what should be our response? There's only one response to this and that is worship; the total commitment of our lives to him who has shouldered everything for us. He and he alone deserves my life.

The Lectures and Seminars

Week 2: The Earth is the Lord's: Ecology and Christian Mission

by Chris Wright

Chris Wright

Chris Wright was born in Belfast, Northern Ireland. His doctorate from Cambridge is in Old Testament ethics. He taught the Old Testament in India for five years at the Union Biblical Seminary, and then returned to the faculty of All Nations Christian College, a missionary training college in England, where he was Principal from 1993-2001. Chris is currently the International Director of Langham Partnership International. He has written several books, including commentaries on Deuteronomy and Ezekiel. An ordained Anglican, on the staff of All Souls Church, Langham Place, London, Chris and his wife Liz have four adult children and three grandchildren, and live in London.

Three Worlds

The Earth is the Lord's: Ecology and Christian Mission

My purpose is to try to lay a biblical foundation for our thinking about this issue. I'm not a scientist, so I'm not here to comment on global warming and everything else. We're all aware of those issues or should be. My purpose is to lay down some biblical foundations as a platform for Christian ecological concern and action, which will give validity and support for all of us as Christian human beings living on this planet, for deciding what we ought to do about it. Those foundations are also to support and validate those Christians who see it to be part of their specific missional calling to be involved in environmental issues. There are a number of Christian organisations for whom that is true. One of the earliest, from an evangelical point of view, is the A Rocha ministries, which works on all continents of the Earth. They see caring for creation as an important dimension of Christian mission, to which they are called.

I want to divide what I have to say into four main sections, of which the first will be the longest. My first main section is to ask, 'What does it mean to say that the Earth belongs to the Lord?' Secondly, we will move on to ask, 'What has gone wrong with the Earth?' Thirdly, we want to recognise that part of our Christian biblical faith is redemptive. God's purpose is the redemption of creation, because it was created to give God glory, and it *will* give God glory. Finally, we want to think about practical aspects of that, in terms of our mission. Is it then right to say that as Christians we should see environmental and ecological concern and action as legitimate and valid parts of the many things to which we are called, in being called into the mission of God?

The Earth: God's gift

God's Earth

I've divided this section into two: on one hand, it is God's Earth, and on the other hand it is also our Earth, because he has put it into our stewardship. It is God's Earth and it's our Earth. The first, of course, is the most fundamental. 'The earth is the LORD's,' says Psalm 24. Or, as Moses puts it in Deuteronomy 10:14: 'To the LORD your God belong the heavens, even the highest heavens, the earth and everything in it.' The Old Testament makes this very bold claim that Yahweh, the God of Israel, owns the universe. There are several dimensions of that, which are also expressed in the Scripture. The first is that creation is good.

Creation is good

The fact that the Earth is good, or the goodness of creation, is one of the most obvious things that's affirmed in Genesis 1 and 2. It's repeated six times and then on the seventh time it's amplified. Now I want to say a few things about that expression, the 'goodness of creation'. First of all, a 'good creation' can only be the work of a good God. This is what sets the biblical Hebrew account of creation in stark contrast to a number of other creation accounts which you get in other Near Eastern cultures. In those you find that the gods of nature are portrayed in various degrees of evil, doing bad things to each other, out of which the creation comes. But in the Old Testament, the creation is fundamentally good, because it is the work of the one good God Yahweh. Creation reflects the character of God.

This is said in a number of places. We are all familiar with Psalm 19: 'The heavens declare the glory of God'. Perhaps we're not quite so familiar with Psalm 50:6, which says 'And the heavens proclaim his righteousness, for God himself is judge' or Psalm 65, which speaks about the Earth witnessing God as Provider. In Acts 14:7, Paul tells the people that the very creation – the sun, the moon, the rain – witness to the kindness of God. And in Romans 1:20, he says creation speaks of the power of God. So the Scriptures show that creation witnesses to the God who made it and reflects something of his character.

Creation is *intrinsically* good. The goodness of creation is independent of us. It's very significant in Genesis, that the affirmations, 'It is good,' were not made by human beings. It is God who says that the creation is good, prior to any human observation or involvement in it. This affirmation of the goodness of creation is God's approval. The created order has value, because God values it. In fact, we take our value, in part, from the fact that we are part of creation, which God values.

The goodness of creation includes change. There's a sense of purposefulness in the way that God makes the creation, such that there can be natural history as well as human history. The goodness of creation includes an eschatological dimension; it is pointing towards the future. Creation is not yet, and was not even when he made it, all that God planned it to be. Creation was made to grow and develop.

Creation is distinct but not independent

Creation is distinct from but still dependent upon God. The opening verse of the Bible says that 'In the beginning God (subject) created (verb) the heavens and the earth (object).' There is a fundamental distinction between God as Creator and everything else, created. There is the being of God, uncreated and ultimate, and there is the being of the created, created by him and contingent upon him. This view that God and the universe are different is an essential part of a Christian biblical world view. It stands out against *monism*, the view that all reality is ultimately one singular thing. It also stands out against *pantheism*, the idea that everything is God, in some sense. The biblical teaching of the creation is that creation is distinct from the Creator, but is still totally dependent upon him. It's not co-eternal, that matter and spirit were always there from the beginning. It's not a self-sustaining bio-system. The Bible portrays the whole universe as distinct from God, but dependent upon him every second. All the time, God is sustaining the creation, and he has built into it an incredible capacity for renewal. That is there because of God's gift, and God's sustaining power. So that's the second thing: distinct, but not independent, dependent on God.

Creation is sacred, but not divine

In the polytheistic religions that surrounded Israel, the different forces of nature, the sun, the rain, the thunder, the rivers, were regarded as divine beings. So you had many religious rituals and magical practices to try to persuade these nature gods to do what you wanted them to do. Nature itself was regarded as divine.

Now the Bible sets itself against all that. These great realities of the world are not divine in themselves. Whatever power they have – and it is great – is the work of Yahweh and under his command. And so the Bible teaches that we are to respect and care for the non-human creation of the world, but we are not to treat it as if it were God. That does not mean that there's no sense of the sacredness of creation. There is a fundamental difference between treating creation as sacred, and treating it as divine: just as there is in the way we talk about the sacredness of human life without meaning that human beings are divine.

The Old Testament constantly treats creation in relation to God. The Bible says creation obeys God, submits to God's command, reveals God's glory, benefits from God's sustaining power, serves God's purposes and constantly relates to God. There is a sacredness, a God-relatedness of the non-human created order which we are called upon to honour. But to worship nature, as in itself God, is a form of idolatry that both the Old and New Testaments condemn. So that's the first big picture, then: the Earth is the Lord's; it is good; distinct from God but not independent; sacred but not divine.

Our Earth

Psalm 115:16 says that the heavens belong to the Lord, but the Earth he has given to the sons of Adam. The Earth is the place of human habitation. It's also the place of non-human habitation – other creatures share the Earth with us. Psalm 104 celebrates this, and yet the Bible never says that the Earth is given to these other creatures in quite the same way as the Earth is given to human beings. So what is it about human beings that makes us unique?

Before we look at what makes human beings special, we need to recognise that the opening chapters of the Bible don't immediately emphasise human uniqueness, but what we have in common with the rest of the creation. Just like all the rest of the animals, humans are blessed. We're instructed to multiply and fill the Earth: so were they. We share the sixth day of creation with the livestock, the wild animals and the creepy-crawlies. The only difference is that man was made from the dust of the ground, which is a distinction that does not obviously mark him out as superior. We're told that God breathed that breath of life into our very nostrils, which speaks of the intimacy of the relationship between God and the human creation, but having the breath of life is not in itself unique.

Image and dominion

We have a lot in common with the rest of creation. Genesis makes that clear. But we are distinct in what respect? Only two things are said about humans in Genesis which are not said about the other creatures. One is that God chose to make us in his own image and secondly, God instructed us to rule over the rest of creation. These are the two aspects of our distinctiveness: the image of God and our dominion. Having made us in his own image (Gen. 1:26) God then gives us this mandate to rule over every living creature on the planet. By making us like himself, God equipped up for this role of authority and rule within creation. The two affirmations clearly go together. It's not that being in the image of God simply is having dominion, but that we were made to be like God, in order that we might rule over the creation. One enables and facilitates the other.

God then instructs the human species not only to fill the Earth – which is what he told the other creatures to do – but also to subdue it and rule over it. That second word, to rule over the Earth, is to exercise dominion. God hands on to human hands this delegated form of his own kingly authority within creation. It's often pointed out that in the ancient world, and indeed the modern world, as we saw in Iraq, people put up huge statues of themselves in different parts of their territory to show who's boss. So when God puts his image in the Earth, it is to say that 'This Earth belongs to God, and here is my image exercising my sovereignty over the Earth.' God installs human beings, as his image, within creation with the authority that belongs to God as the Creator. Human dominion reflects God's kingship. But the image of God, then, is not a licence for abuse based on arrogant supremacy.

Servant kingship

When you look at the stories of kingship in the Old Testament, the whole idea of kingship in Israel was to serve the people. Many of them didn't, many became just like pagan kings, but remember what the elders said to the young king Rehoboam, when he was asking their advice on how he should rule after Solomon. They said to him (1 Kgs. 12:7): 'If you will be a servant to this people today and serve them, and speak good words to them when you answer them, then they will be your servants forever.' Mutual servanthood was the vision of kingship. It was the duty of the people to serve and obey the king, but it was his primary duty to serve them and care for their needs; to provide justice and protection. Human dominion is to be modelled on the servanthood model that God has given us. This is precisely the model that we see in the Lord Jesus Christ. He exercises his kingship through loving generosity, self-sacrifice and care, and that is the Christlike pattern for the way in which we are to exercise our leadership. This is the way we should be behaving in creation. We're to exercise rule (Gen. 1), through servanthood and caring responsibility (Gen. 2).

The Earth: Curse and covenant

God's curse on the Earth

Things did not stay the way God intended them to be. When human beings chose to rebel against their Creator (Gen. 3), the impact was felt throughout the whole physical environment. The most poignant expression is the language of God's curse. God's words to Adam were, 'Cursed is the ground because of you'. The particular Hebrew word *adama* can mean the whole Earth, but it more commonly means the surface of the Earth, the soil. How could it have been otherwise, given that we are creatures of the Earth?

There are those who ask the question, is creation itself fallen, in some sense? Is there moral evil at work within the processes of the non-human creation, as there obviously is within human hearts and human society? Or is God's curse on the Earth ontological, affecting the very nature and being of the planet? Or is it primarily functional, affecting our human relationship with the Earth and the way in which the Earth responds to us as its human rulers?

Some want to argue for an ontological understanding of the Fall and nature, and attribute all natural phenomena which cause suffering or pain to the Fall, an expression of the curse. Serious Christian theologians say that but I'm not sure. Part of the difficulty is that many of those natural phenomena appear to have been there before human beings existed – and that is a controversial statement. I agree with those who see those features of the natural order not as symptoms of sin in themselves, but as part of the not-yet-perfect nature of God's creation from the beginning. It's worth reminding ourselves that when God made the Earth, back in Genesis, the whole Earth was not the Garden of Eden. The Garden of Eden was a safe environment within the Earth, into which God put the first human beings. The implication would seem to be that the task of subduing the Earth would begin there and work outwards, because the Earth itself was far from subdued. I don't think we should imagine that the whole Earth was a perfect paradise at that time, in which all the forces of nature were as we might wish them to be, and everything was only disturbed by human sin. However, whether ontological or functional, we live in a cursed Earth, whatever that might finally mean. Human sin has affected human creation in all kinds of ways.

God's covenant with the Earth

We must never interpret Genesis 3 without also recognising what is said in the covenant with Noah, clearly represents a fresh start for creation. Much of the language in Genesis 1 reoccurs in Genesis 8 and 9: God sends Noah and his family out with explicit words of blessing, with explicit commands to go forth and to fill the Earth. And in that context, God makes his covenant with creation. It's not just a covenant with human beings: the covenant goes to every living being on the planet. God binds himself in a covenant commitment to life on Earth, and in that sense we stand on the same platform as all the rest of the creatures on the planet. By implication that creates a sense of obligation and responsibility at a horizontal level as well, because when God made his covenant with Israel, it's not just that the Israelites were vertically bound with God, they were also horizontally committed to one another within that covenantal relationship. God expects us to behave towards the rest of creation within the boundaries of that covenantal relationship which binds us both to God. It's also described as an eternal covenant, so it is cosmic in its scope and in its duration.

So we live in a covenanted Earth, as well as a cursed Earth, and the implication of that at an ethical and social level is that there is a connection in biblical thinking between the way we behave in society and how things happen ecologically. Justice on Earth is closely integrated with harmony in nature in biblical thinking. It's a common belief that you can find in other cultures as well. There seems to be this primal recognition in human societies that the way we behave towards one another is going to have an impact on the way the world behaves in relation to us.

The positive implications
If you look at Psalm 72, the writer prays that the king will give good government and do justice for the poor, but the expectation woven within that is there will be order and prosperity in the natural realm. It's also seen eschatologically in Isaiah 11 and 32: when the Messiah comes and there will be righteous government under this righteous king, then there will also be global, environmental peace and blessing. So positively, one of the things that we might want to say to our governments is that if they care about ecology, then do justice. If they persist in injustice, then the Earth suffers.

The negative implications

If you look at Hosea, he perceives the ecological effects of human sin and makes a damning list of social evils – idolatry, murder, adultery, lying, lack of integrity, injustice. Then he finishes, 'Because of this the land mourns' (Hos. 4:1–3). It isn't purely metaphorical: he recognises that when human beings wilfully abandon the knowledge and the ways of God, the effects are wider than merely human.

The Earth: glory and redemption

This is another great reality which Christians, particularly evangelical Christians overlook. We are very good in our environmental concern, looking back to creation, but not quite as good at looking forward. But the glory of the Earth and its redemption are also very strong theological motivations for ecological concern.

God's glory is the goal of redemption

I learned the shorter catechism as a boy, and I remember the very first question: 'What is the chief end of man?' The answer is, 'to glorify God and enjoy him forever.' The same question and answer could be given biblically about creation as a whole. The creation exists for the praise and glory of its Creator God, and for mutual enjoyment. God enjoys his creation, and the creation praises and enjoys God. Part of our goal in life as human beings – to glorify God and enjoy him – is not something uniquely human; it's something that we share with the whole of creation. Of course, we do it in uniquely human ways: we praise our Creator with our hearts, minds, hands and voices, and all the things that God has given us (rationality, emotion, language, art and music). The Bible tells us that the rest of creation also praises God, and can be summoned repeatedly to do it. I don't know how the creation praises God, nor do I understand how God receives the praise of his non-human creation, but just because I can't understand it, doesn't mean that it doesn't happen. The Bible affirms that the whole of creation praises God and will one day join us in praise to God.

Creation exists to bring glory to God, and one of the connections the Bible often makes is between 'the glory of God' and 'the fullness of creation'. The Bible proceeds from emptiness to fullness in the story of creation; the water, land and sky are created and then filled with fish and birds and animals. There's something about this incredible richness of the creation that also brings glory to God. The fullness of the Earth is God's glory. The glory of God is in part constituted by the fullness of the Earth. This incredible richness of creation reflects and is part of the glory of God within it.

God's redemption includes the whole of creation

Again, as evangelical Christians, we're not terribly good at this, because we often talk about our great desire to be with God in heaven, and we look forward to living with God in some other place, when the Bible tells us very clearly that God's intention is a new creation. This creation is not headed for some cosmic incinerator, and that's it, finished. That provides an eschatological vision for our ecological concern now. It's not just that we should care for the Earth because God made it (looking backwards): we should care for the Earth because God is going to redeem it. It's God's future. The final vision of the Bible is not of us floating off to heaven, but of God coming here to redeem this Earth. God dwelling with us is the final vision of the Scriptures, in a redeemed, purged world of creation, all the evil sucked out of it and the curse finished. Basically, the whole point of Christian eschatology – looking to the future – is to say, if that is what God plans for the future, how should we live now? That's true of personal ethics. And if God's planet Earth is destined for redemption and recreation, then we should be caring for it in the present.

The Earth: our mission

It's one thing to say that we have this biblical teaching about creation, about the glory of God in creation, about God caring about creation, about how we should care for it as human beings, but is it a legitimate part of Christian mission? I want to answer yes, for at least three positive reasons and a negative one, a desperately urgent issue in our contemporary world. Only someone who is wilfully blind could ignore the depressing list of the destruction of creation: pollution; the extinction of species; the loss of soil; the depletion of ozone and climate change. All these things are there! If we are faced now with some of these horrific facts of the suffering of the Earth itself, we must ask how does God respond to this abuse of his creation? If God cares about his creation to the extent of knowing when a sparrow falls to the Earth, as Jesus said, how much more should we care for that creation, given the extent of the knowledge we have?

Love and obedience

Our care for creation should flow from love for the Creator and obedience to his command. 'The first and greatest commandment in the laws,' says Jesus, 'is love the Lord your God with all your heart and with all your soul and all your strength.' In our human experience, we know that to love somebody is to care for what belongs to them, and if the Bible affirms that the Earth belongs to Christ who made it, to take care of the Earth for Christ's sake is surely a dimension of our calling to love God. I find it quite inexplicable that there are Christians who claim to love God, to be disciples of Jesus and yet have no concern for the Earth. Jesus said, 'If you love me, keep my commandments,' and the very first commandment that we have in the Bible is to care for the Earth. God will call us to account for our humanity as much as our Christianity.

Kings and priests

Caring for creation is a return to the proper exercise of our kingly and priestly role within creation. Some might say, 'Where does that come from?' Greg Beale and others have argued that when you look at the Tabernacle, the Temple in the Old Testament, it looks both backwards and forwards. It is a picture of the dwelling place of God, as it were, between heaven and Earth, but it also points forward to the great picture of revelation, when the whole creation will be the dwelling place of God. Genesis 1 and 2 told us that we were put into the creation to rule and to serve; that's the function of kingship and priesthood. Serving and keeping the Tabernacle were the prime tasks of the priests. So human beings are put into the Earth with this combined job of ruling and serving, it is our quintessential role in creation. So when we come to the new creation, how significant is it that Revelation tells us explicitly that because of the saving work of Christ in the new creation, we will be restored to be kings and priests on Earth, under God? The Earth is waiting to receive again not only its Lord Jesus Christ but its truly human kings and priests to run the world as God intended it.

Compassion and justice

Caring for the planet is a legitimate part of Christian mission because it embodies two elements which are intrinsic to all Christian mission: compassion and justice. These are at the very heart of Christian obedience, and they are both also part of the reality of those who care for creation. Compassion, first of all: to care for God's creation is essentially an unselfish form of love, exercised for the sake of creatures who cannot repay you. It reflects the same quality of the love of God who, in spite of us not loving him, chose to love us. And finally it is also a matter of justice, one of the other big biblical words. Environmental action is often a case of defending the weak against the strong, the defenceless against the powerful, the violated against the attacker, the voiceless against the stridency of the greedy. Those are what characterise the justice of God.

So perhaps it's not surprising when you come to what Proverbs says about the definition of a righteous person, that the righteous person is not the only one who (Prov. 29:7) 'cares about justice for the poor', but he also (Prov. 12:10) 'cares for the needs of his animal.' That's also the mark of righteousness. Biblical mission is as holistic as biblical righteousness; not just because it cares for the whole needs for whole people, but it cares for the whole of God's creation, because God's ultimate purpose is the redemption of his whole creation.

Week 3: Matters of life and death
by Dr John Wyatt

Dr John Wyatt

John Wyatt is Professor of Neonatal Paediatrics at University College London, and Chairman of the Study Group of the Christian Medical Fellowship. He has been a frequent contributor to political, media and academic debates on controversial ethical issues. He and his family are members of All Souls Church in London. His book, *Matters of Life and Death*, is published by InterVarsity Press.

Matters of life and death

How on earth does this wonderful spiritual teaching actually engage in the real world, in the nitty-gritty? Today I'm going to be talking about some controversial, difficult and painful things, some of the things you don't normally get in church; like abortion, infertility, sex, old age, Alzheimer's disease, disability and death.

As Christian people, we've got to build a bridge between the world of the Christian faith, the world of the Bible, and the secular world in which God has placed us. I haven't got a set of slick and easy answers for difficult problems. I genuinely don't believe there are any easy answers, but I do want to suggest some ways of thinking about these topics which I hope will be helpful.

First of all, I want to stress two important principles. First, virtually every issue to do with bioethics starts with human pain. It's not usually mad scientists who want to play God for the heck of it. No, it is people facing tragedy, who bleed, suffer and struggle, who desperately want to find a solution to their problem, their agony – whatever it costs. So we mustn't talk about these issues – like abortion, euthanasia – with harshness, hatred or judgement in our voices. I sometimes hear Christian people talking about these issues with a harsh rhetoric – talking about the 'slaughter of the innocents', or the 'baby murderers'. I believe this kind of harsh language doesn't help. It just twists the knife in the hearts of so many people who are touched by these issues. Instead, we should talk about them with tears in our eyes. We're called to empathise, to enter into the experience of suffering people, to experience their pain; for costly empathy is the way of Christ. Secondly, we have to realise these are not just issues out there in a sinful society. We are all human beings; we are all touched by the fragility, the vulnerability of our humanity.

I have worked most of my life as a neo-natal paediatrician, in a highly technological and sophisticated intensive care unit in central London. We care for between four and five hundred babies a year, many of which are born right on the limits of viability, or before it. We've seen babies survive at just 22 or 23 weeks of gestation: only five months of pregnancy, instead of the usual nine. We invest a huge amount of time and energy and love and money in trying to help these babies survive. There's a team of over a hundred specialised nursing and medical staff. And it costs money, too: £1,200 per baby per day to provide this kind of care. The total cost to save a premature baby life these days could be easily over £100,000, all paid for by the NHS.

Why do we as a society spend all this time, money and energy? It's because we believe human life is precious. We believe that it is worth it; every baby deserves the chance for survival. And yet, in the same hospital, you'll find another specialist hospital department: the foetal medicine unit, where sophisticated technology is used to detect subtle abnormalities in unborn babies. The abnormalities that are detected are genetic, like Down's syndrome. 90 per cent of people who discover that their babies have Down's syndrome choose abortion. In fact, the whole purpose of the screening process is to detect abnormalities in order to offer choices (so-called) to pregnant women and their partners. Sometimes I and my colleagues, working on the ground floor, are called to speak to people, perhaps a pregnant mother, considering ending the life of a baby who is much more developed compared with the baby we are struggling to save. How can it be that in a modern hospital, you seem to be doing two completely contradictory things? The answer is: modern hospitals are here to do what people want. We don't call them patients any more, we call them 'healthcare consumers'. I am called a 'healthcare provider', and we are here to do what our healthcare consumers want.

The philosophers call it autonomy: I *choose* what is right for me, I make the rules. Welcome to the world of modern healthcare.

What are the forces?

How do we respond to this world as Christians? First of all, we have to try to understand what are the forces, the underlying trends that lie behind the world of modern healthcare, and then we have to try to build a Christian response. I want to very briefly talk about four major social issues in modern healthcare and the way in which they're changing the world in which we live.

Machine thinking

Here's our old friend Richard Dawkins, the high priest of reductionism: 'We are all machines built by DNA whose purpose is to make more copies of the same DNA . . . This is exactly what we are for. We are machines of propagating DNA . . . It is every living object's sole reason for living.'

Historians of medicine have noted how doctors have always taken the best scientific understanding of the world at the time and applied it to the human body. The ancient Greek doctors lived in a world that was made out of earth, wood, wind, fire and water. So, if you have too much fire: that's a fever. If you have too much water, that's oedema – you swell up. If you have too much wind . . . you get the idea.

The Victorians were great engineers. In particular, they invented the science of hydraulics, and they used it to develop steam engines, pumps and drainage systems. And lo and behold, the Victorian doctors discovered that the body is all hydraulics. Now we live in a world that's been transformed by machines, and especially information-processing machines, and lo and behold, the body is an information processing machine.

Technology

Machine thinking is very important to modern healthcare. It's useful because it means we can use technology to change our bodies. If our body is just a machine, then I can repair it when it goes wrong, but also I can improve on its design. If human suffering is the problem, then technology is the answer. Technology offers us the dream of overcoming the fundamental problems of humanity. Just take this list: infertility, unwanted babies, disability and so on . . . These problems have been with us since the dawn of time, they're part of what philosophers call the human condition. But now things are different. We don't have to accept the humanity that has just evolved by random forces over a million years, we can change the design. In fact, there's a whole new movement called trans-humanism, or post-humanism, which is dedicated to enhancing and improving on human design: extending life-span, improving brains, improving techniques.

Ethical relativism

Ethical relativism says there's no such things as absolute right or wrong. Each one of us has a right to choose or invent a moral code that we can live by. Many philosophers are arguing that autonomy is the fundamental guiding principle in all medical ethics, everything else is footnotes. Autonomy is king.

Consumerism

Consumerism is rampant in healthcare. Consumerism is at heart a spiritual problem, it's idolatry in spiritual terms – it's to put oneself on the throne instead of God. I have the right to choose or invent a lifestyle, not just deciding what is right and wrong, but deciding my entire lifestyle to meet my needs. And it's you: the government, society, the NHS, that has the responsibility of providing what I want. So healthcare turns itself into a modern industry. It's a bit like Tesco: we have the people coming, we try to work out what they want, and then we try to meet their needs. We have targets, we have efficiency savings, we try to improve quality, we're a modern service industry. But what is fascinating and dangerous is that these forces are combining together into a very potent brew.

Consumerism says, 'I want', and relativism says 'Why not?' Technology says 'We can make it happen, but it'll cost you.' Technology always comes at a cost, and sometimes the cost –

personal and spiritual – is much higher than we'd imagine. What's the answer to the high rate of unwanted teenage pregnancies in the UK? What's the answer to world overpopulation? We've got a technological fix, and it's called abortion. It's a typically male response. Think of someone you know who's had a crisis pregnancy. Think of all the complex social, psychological, relational, emotional and spiritual issues that are tied up in that one example. What's the solution? Ten minutes, general anaesthetic, you won't feel a thing, we can do it in your lunch-hour and then it's gone, start again, clean slate. You can get back to work in the afternoon, no one need ever know. Do we really think that is a solution? Many women are profoundly traumatised by what was meant to be a simple, neat solution. Sometimes there's lifelong distress and unresolved grief, not just for women but men also. A number of highly reputable studies have shown that following abortion there is an increased risk of infertility, pelvic infection, premature labour in subsequent pregnancies, depression, self-harm and suicide. So much for the simple, cost-free fix.

The rate of abortion is rising steadily year on year in the UK. It's the despair of the health-planners. Last year, there were over two hundred thousand abortions in the UK. In the same year there were over six hundred thousand babies born. This means that about one in four of every established pregnancy in 2008 is going to end in an abortion. Do you know where the most dangerous place for children in the UK is? In their mother's womb. What is happening in our society? Up to one in three of every woman of child-bearing age has had an abortion, and yet it is never talked about, it's like a hidden scar running through our society – damaging, twisting, affecting lives. It's one of the major ways in which the evil one has his grip on our society, with its untold consequences.

I also want to highlight a wonderful, Christian response to this issue, which is already making a profound difference. Whenever we say that something is wrong, we must immediately say 'Here is a better way.' The Holy Spirit has moved the hearts of many affected by these issues, who have had abortions, who found healing as Christians and are then moving out in compassion, setting up centres, often called Crisis Pregnancy Centres. There are over 160 centres, linked into Care. You can find out about them on www.Care-Confidential.com.

Prenatal screening

There are other technical fixes: prenatal screening is a technological solution for disability. How are we going to reduce the number of disabled children in our society? We have the answer: we can get rid of those unwanted individuals. It's sometimes called 'the prevention of genetic diseases', but of course it's not prevention, it's the destruction of individuals. It's the only answer I know in medicine where doctors offer to treat a disease by getting rid of the individuals who have it. Glen McGee, an American philosopher, goes further, and argues that in some situations, if there's a genetic problem in an unborn baby, there is a 'duty' to have an abortion.

Here's an ominous progression. When the Abortion Act came in, we had abortion available in extreme circumstances; an argument based on compassion. Then with women's liberation and feminism, it becomes abortion as an option: an argument based on liberation. Now it becomes a duty to abort: an argument based on social responsibility. Sometimes, if somebody is pushing a buggy with a baby in it which has some obvious genetic disorder, it used to be the response from people was 'How sad.' These days, you may get the same response, but you may get 'How could you *choose* to have a baby like that?' God-like knowledge brings us God-like responsibility.

There are many other examples of the way in which medical technology is being used as a solution to profound human problems: *in vitro* fertilization, embryonic selection, therapeutic cloning: all of these are being actively promoted as technical solutions. At the other end of life, euthanasia or what is sometimes called 'physician-assisted suicide' is the same thing: a quick technological fix to the problem of suffering and disability.

How can we find a Christian and biblical response?

Biblical ethics, the way we treat one another, comes from biblical anthropology, the way we are made. So what does the Bible teach us about the way we're made? I want to highlight three foundational, biblical concepts.

Designed to reflect God

Biologists and anthropologists are fascinated by the question of what it means to be a human being. It turns out that we share 98.4% of our DNA with a chimpanzee. And amazingly, a whole group of scientists have become fascinated by the remaining 1.6%. If we can only work out what that 1.6% is, then at last we'll understand what it means to be a human being. But it turns out we share 95% of our DNA with a rat. And we share about 70% with a fruit fly, and 50% with an oak tree.

Human beings are not self-explanatory. We derive our meaning from outside ourselves. We are not autonomous individuals. We are reflections of another reality: the character and being of God himself. Human beings are God-like human beings. The purpose of our humanity, the structure of our lives, only makes sense in light of our creation in God's image.

From dust you are made

The Bible is clear that we are made out of dust. We're made out of the same stuff as everything else. We share the limitations of the physical universe. And so, in God's design, we are meant to be physical, independent, frail and vulnerable beings. This is not an accident. It's part of the design. God could have made us differently, but in his infinite and gentle wisdom he chose to put his majestic image into a creature made of dust. So, in Christian thinking, dependence is not an evil, outrageous, subhuman thing. It does not rob us of our dignity. To the secular philosopher, dependence is a terrible threat because it robs us of our autonomy. But in Christian thinking, dependence is part of the narrative of human life. You come into the world totally dependent on the love and care of others. The very fact that you are sitting there, now, today is only because somebody loved you when you were born. And then we go through a phase of life when others depend on us. And most of us are going to end our lives totally dependent on the love and care of others. This does not rob us of our dignity or humanity. It is part of the narrative of human life.

Made into a family

In God's design for humanity, we are dependent beings. But also making love and making babies belongs together. It's not an accident that the most intimate expression of union that two human beings are capable of is also the way that we make babies. In secular thinking, there's no connection. Making love is sex, that's like a recreational activity, it's fun. Making babies: that's serious. The two things are totally different, but in God's thinking, making love and making babies are locked together. DNA is the means by which a unique love between a woman and a man is converted into a baby. It enshrines the countless conjunctions of your ancestors, the myriad love-makings of which you are composed. The reason your nose is that shape and your toes go down, and so on, is because of all those people who made love and made babies, since the dawn of time. And that's why for adopted children, the task of tracing their physical parents' genetic roots may be so significant. Whatever our environment, however we're brought up, we can never escape the reality of our physical structure. Our genetic structure expresses the web of relationships out of which each of us is being created. That's the way God planned it. That's the way it was meant to be.

On one level, an embryo is just a bundle of cells, a collection of cellular machinery. But at the same time, God is bringing out – calling into existence – a unique person, a wonderful new being made in God's image. How those two things hold together, I haven't a clue. But what I do know, is that they're both true, and we have to hold them together. We hold the physical and the immaterial together. And we hold together that God has already called this person into being, and they are not yet what God has planned for them. But at what point in development does the human person start? Is it when the brain begins to develop? Is it when the baby starts to kick? You can't use science to reveal at which point God is calling a unique human person into existence.

So we're made to reflect God's image, we're made out of dust and we're made into a family. You know, geneticists have been going around the world, collecting DNA from every conceivable population group around the planet. They've compared all the DNA and come to the conclusion that every single human being is descended from a single male ancestor and a single female ancestor, and they lived somewhere in North Africa or the Middle East, and the current timing is somewhere between 150,000 and 80,000 years ago. This is now becoming a scientific consensus. In genetic reality, we're all a single family, and therefore we treat even strangers, immigrants or aliens, with respect, dignity and love. And in a family, the strong have a duty to protect the weak.

Part of being a family is to be dependent on each other. We're dependent beings and to think otherwise, to make independence our project, is to live a lie. Part of our design is to be a burden to one another. I'm supposed to be a burden to you, and you're supposed to be a burden to me. Paul in Galatians tells us that's how we fulfil Christ's plan for our lives: 'Bear one another's burdens, and so fulfil the law of Christ.' That's the way God planned it.

There's a curious ambiguity in the Bible about physical death. Death is both a judgement for sin, but also evidence of God's grace, it is a severe mercy. In the Genesis narrative, after Adam and Eve have fallen, they're expelled from the Garden and God places cherubim on a flaming sword to prevent them from seeking re-entry into the Garden. Why? To stop them entering into the Garden in their fallen state and eating the fruit of the tree of life and living forever. Because living forever in a fallen state is not a blessing, it's a curse. Human life is shortened by God, not just out of judgement, but also out of grace. So in God's grace, death can become a strange form of healing. There are some situations which are so awful, so twisted by sin, so affected by the Fall, that it seems that only death can bring ultimate healing.

One of the terrible consequences of the Fall is the suffering – terrible, inexplicable, protracted suffering. And how do we respond?

Thank God that over the last fifty years, he's given us scientific and medical knowledge to control pain in a variety of new approaches. The whole speciality of palliative care was created almost entirely by Christian doctors and nurses who wished to use their God-given skills to help people die well. It's a wonderful example of practical, innovative, compassionate Christian response. But there's no quick, technological fix to the problem of suffering.

Suffering is not a question which demands an answer, it's not a problem which demands a solution. It's a mystery which demands a presence. God doesn't explain the mystery of evil and suffering, he enters into it. The Incarnation is the greatest example of empathy the cosmos has ever seen. That is Christ's example to us. We enter into the mystery of suffering. How does God come, when he breaks into human history? Does he throw away that old, failed version of humanity, and start again with a completely new design? No, God comes to us in the form of an original model, made out of dust like the rest of us. God himself took on our humanity and became a totally dependent baby. But because Jesus was a baby, then all babies are special and I'm called to treat this little being, struggling for life in the intensive care unit with the same wonder, the same respect that Mary and Joseph treated their little bundle two thousand years ago.

As Jesus pays the ultimate price for our salvation on the cross, at the end of his life, his hands and legs are stretched out, he is totally dependent, totally vulnerable, and through his cracked lips he croaks, 'I am thirsty.' So we can learn from this that dependence does not destroy our fundamental dignity. To depend on others for all your bodily needs is part of the experience which God himself has entered into. And if it's good enough for Jesus, it's good enough for us. There is no human experience you can go through which Christ himself has not experienced. He was with us in the womb, as he will be with us in the tomb. Are you facing some new crisis? A new diagnosis? A new future? Some new terror? Know that Christ has been there before, and will be with you.

In the person of the risen Jesus, we see God's final vote of confidence in the original human model. So our humanity is not a barrier that comes between us and God. No, it's the very means by which God is revealed. God's plan for us is not to become less human and more spiritual. No, his plan is for us to become fully human. Totally human, like the Lord Jesus himself.

Just as I come to the close, I want to point out the hope. Christian caring never stops at the agony of the cross. It is shot through with hope, anticipation and longing for the future. And that's all to do with agape love: it means 'respect love'. Respect love is different from worldly love. Respect love builds you up. When we care for a profoundly disabled person, for a dying child, for an Alzheimer's sufferer with genuine respect, with agape love, we are pointing towards the future. Paul in Corinthians 1 says, 'Love never fails.' It seems that in some mysterious way, the acts of genuine agape love, which demonstrate Christlike caring in this world, will somehow remain. They will become part of the new heaven and the new Earth.

Finally there's something even more amazing. God comes into the Earth and takes on a physical body, made out of physical atoms. Carbon, phosphorous, mitochondria, cell membranes become part of his body. And when he's raised and goes to glory, those physical atoms have gone, transformed into a new kind of reality. And then in the age to come, when our bodies are raised from the dead, the physical molecules of carbon and phosphorous from which we're composed will be transformed like his. That's the way God planned it. That's the way God wanted it to be. By God's grace he will help us to be the people, to become the ones he wanted us to be.

Science at the beginning of life (Seminar)

Introduction

These are issues which touch all of us very profoundly and, whenever we talk about these issues, we must talk about them with sensitivity. I'm very conscious of the fact that many people sitting in this room may have been affected. I'm going to talk a bit about what's called reproductive technology, some of the political events that have been going on and try to develop some Christian responses.

Creating a baby

When I went to medical school, the section on how to make babies was very short and I knew it all. But nowadays it's quite different. To make a baby in 2008 you need several things and there isn't necessarily any connection at all between them. You need a source of human eggs – and it's possible to get eggs: if you give hormones to a woman, you can stimulate the ovaries so that instead of producing one egg every month, they will actually produce up to twenty eggs and then you can 'harvest' the eggs, and put them in a glass dish. Then you need sperm and there are a number of ways of obtaining sperm. The sperm and the egg are mixed together in a glass dish and eventually you end up with a one cell embryo.

The one cell divides into two cells and then four and then eight, and so on, becoming a bundle of cells called a blastocyst. Normally the process of human fertilisation happens in the fallopian tube: the sperm passes up through the cervix, the womb and the fallopian tube and meets the egg. Fertilisation takes place and this little bundle of cells is then wafted down the fallopian tube until it enters into the cavity of the womb, where implantation takes place. It then beds itself into the lining of the womb which has been prepared in the monthly cycle and then it starts to grow like a little parasite and develops its own blood supply.

At eight weeks, if you see this in real life, what strikes you is the tiny little foetus is moving and thrashing around vigorously. The kidneys are producing urine and all the main bodily structures are complete. At fifteen weeks, the baby is sucking and swallowing, the fingers are moving and the baby will respond to sound. Science has shown that babies in the womb are much more interactive and responsive than was ever realised: the unborn baby responds to the mother's voice, tastes the amniotic fluid, can detect sound, movement, even light within the womb.

When the Psalmist wrote Psalm 139, 'My frame was not hidden from you when I was woven together in the depths of the Earth,' at that time they knew nothing about what was going on in the womb. Now with ultrasound, we can see what nobody's ever seen before. We can see into this hidden creation chamber, we can see the baby being formed into a living breathing human person.

But of course it is possible to use our knowledge in other ways. Scientists are fascinated by embryos. From that single cell, you have over two hundred completely different types of cells: brain cells, skin cells, kidney cells, sperm, eggs: all sorts of cells and yet they all came from that one cell embryo. It has all the genetic information that goes to make up every single cell within the human body – and that's why scientists are fascinated by the human embryo. If you can only learn how the human embryo creates all those cells, then we could have an infinite supply of kidney cells to repair kidneys, brain cells to repair brains, skin cells for burns and so on.

Regenerative medicine

So there's this whole new form of medicine which is called regenerative medicine. It's the idea of using the healing properties within the body itself for the purposes of medicine. Fundamentally I see the whole idea of regenerative medicine as a very Christian, biblical idea. God has locked within the body fantastic healing and repairing properties. Do you know that when you're eighteen, you are working at a hundred per cent repairing efficiency? When you're eighteen you can just about live forever. Within the body the repair mechanisms are so incredible that whatever the damage, you're able to repair that damage. Once you get to nineteen, your repair mechanisms start to be less than a hundred per cent fully effective and gradually, bit by bit, the damage starts to accumulate in your body. By the time you get to my age, the fact that my repair mechanisms are not working properly is all too obvious. Death occurs when your repair mechanisms are so useless that eventually the body gives up the unequal struggle and you die.

So from a medical point of view, if only we could understand how these repair mechanisms work, if only we could make them work better and control them, then we would have huge potential for good: restoring, repairing and recreating damaged limbs, damaged organs and so on. But the question is, where do we find the stem cells? How can we do this? As Paul says, we don't do evil in order that good may obtain. That's a fundamental Christian principle: we mustn't do evil in order that good can come from it.

This is an area of painful controversy among Christians and I have to be honest and say that there are some Christian people who feel that because the status of the embryo is uncertain, therefore it is appropriate to destroy an embryo in the belief that a greater good can come from it. But I don't. There are other sources of stem cells and there are many different kinds of stem cell. If you read the papers, you'll get the idea that the only way of getting stem cells is by destroying embryos. It's presented in the media as though medicine has run into a terrible road block, there's no hope ahead, we've got all these terrible diseases, the only hope forward is to destroy embryos. I have to say it is completely, utterly false.

The reality in medicine is not like that at all. There are other ways of getting stem cells which are already being used and which are being spectacularly successful. A bone marrow transplant is a stem cell treatment. In fact there are more than seventy therapies currently entering into medicine which are using stem cells but none of them, not one, uses stem cells that are taken from embryos. They're stem cells taken from the bone marrow, from umbilical cord blood, from other different places in the body. This is a massive area of research which is already saving lives, leading to great advances, and I see this whole thing as a wonderful way in which scientists are thinking God's thoughts after him. We don't need to destroy embryos. Embryonic stem cells are scientifically interesting but it's probably at least twenty years before any kind of therapy might come from them. And there are lots of risks associated with embryonic stem cells, in particular that they might turn into tumours and create other problems.

So why is the whole agenda being pushed forward? Three powerful lobby groups have got together and have very successfully pushed forward the whole process of embryo testing and embryonic stem cell research. Group one is the scientists – there's a whole bunch of scientists who see an option of getting Nobel prizes and huge programme grants and therefore this is a way of pushing forward the scientific agenda. Secondly, there's a group of commercial people: biotechnology companies, start-up companies – there's huge commercial interest in this. If somebody could crack a way of repairing human pancreases or something else like that, think of the money you could make. And thirdly, the government sees a fantastic way that we can steal a march on the rest of the world. The rest of the world has banned embryonic stem cell research, pretty well. If the UK government allows it, then we will attract inward investment, we'll attract scientists from the rest of the world, we can steal a march on the rest of the world. Those three groups have done an incredibly successful job at presenting to the media and to the country as a whole the idea that the essential way forward for medical research is by the wholesale destruction of embryos.

Foetal testing

Another issue which is rapidly advancing is this idea that we can test the unborn baby for genetic abnormalities, This is called prenatal genetic testing and this has grown into a huge industry. And interestingly the whole nature of pregnancy has changed.

Again, when I first went to medical school, none of this existed and basically when you were pregnant, if this was a wanted baby, then pregnancy was a fun time. You enjoyed the fact that you were pregnant. But these days, for many people, pregnancy is turned into an experience of anxiety. 'What tests should I have? I've just been for this test and they tell me I've got a one in two hundred and eighty-three chance of some rare genetic disorder. They say if I have a further test, that might actually damage or even destroy my baby.' Many people don't tell anybody that they're pregnant until they've had all the tests to make sure that the baby is healthy, because they know that they might have to have an abortion. And some sociologists have come up with the idea of 'the tentative pregnancy'. The idea is that I don't actually allow myself to 'bond' – to develop an emotional relationship with my unborn baby – because I might have to walk away.

The whole rhetoric is that 'Our purpose is simply to offer you choice; we're here to say "Do you want this baby? Is this the sort of baby you wish to have?" We're here to offer you choices.' But is the rhetoric of choice appropriate for parents? You're given what you're given and in God's plan, you have this wonderful little baby and you fall in love. They take your heart and then over the next eighteen years, you discover all the revolting and terrible characteristics of this child but by then it's much too late, you've already fallen in love with them. Technology turns it round. I learn that they might have this and that problem before I've met them.

Are we related?

Then there's the whole question of the genetic relationships. When an egg is donated to another woman who then carries the baby, whose baby is it? Who is the mother? There's the whole legal problem about whose baby it is and the question of genetic medical information. This baby will face risks that are different from the risks that the mother has, because the baby isn't genetically related to the carrying mother. In fact, because over one percent of all children in our country are being born by *in vitro* fertilisation, many created by egg and sperm donation, so a young person in our society today could meet this wonderful other young person and to fall in love with her and it's perfectly possible that they are actually half siblings, genetically related. If they did have children together there would be a huge risk of some kind of genetic disorder. So the government – the Human Fertilisation Embryonic Authority (HFEA) – has come up with a wonderfully bureaucratic solution. When you fall in love with someone, before you marry them, you send off to the HFEA and say, 'I've just fallen in love with Miss P Smith of 12 Acacia Avenue. I would like to know if I am related to her.' They will then search their database to tell you whether or not you are related.

Abortion

The total number of abortions in the country was, in 2006, 201,000. There are about 600,000 babies a year born so it's one abortion for every three babies that are born alive. There are some uncertainties about these statistics but the information about abortions is collected very carefully in our country. It's one of the positive things about the Abortion Act. What these statistics show is that the caricature of an abortion happening to some teenager of fourteen, in some desperate social circumstances, actually just isn't true. The majority of abortions happen to people in their twenties, many relatively well off. A quarter are married or in stable relationships. And the statistics suggest that less than 1 per cent are carried out for so-called medical reasons: the really hard cases, where the mother's life is at risk, are actually incredibly rare. All those kinds of cases that are always brought up in debate represent a very tiny minority of the abortions that are currently carried out in the UK.

I'm going to skip through to the medical consequences of abortion. There is strong clear evidence that abortion does terrible damage to women. My wife helps to run a crisis pregnancy centre in Islington. When she started, her overriding motivation was to protect unborn babies and although she still sees the need to protect the unborn baby, increasingly she sees the terrible damage done to women by abortion. Unfortunately, despite all that, there are groups in our society who are trying to make the abortion laws even more liberal: it's as though there is just this desperate desire to make abortion easier, to make it more common.

How do we respond?

So this is the world in which God has put us. How on earth do we respond? It does seem to me that the Bible stresses that, first of all, the baby is created by God. It's not an automatic, random process that is going on in the womb. God is lovingly calling into existence a unique being, a being he knows and loves and has known before the foundation of the world; one whom he has intended to reflect his character in a unique way.

There are six billion plus human beings on the planet. Why are there so many? Perhaps it's because each one of us carries some unique reflection of God's image. God has created all these reflections of himself and because God is so big, even six billion people aren't enough to reflect all the characteristics, all the wonderful nature of our Father. God is in covenant with the unborn baby: whenever God calls, he calls by name: even the unborn baby is named, known and loved.

The corruption of language

Even the language we use is important. One of the very interesting themes in human medical ethics is the way that corruption of language proceeds corruption of behaviour. The language we use alters the way we respond. When you talk about the human embryo, the emphasis is on the embryo: there are fruit fly embryos and mouse embryos and dog embryos and rabbit embryos and human embryos and they all look exactly the same because they're all embryos. But if you turn the language round, there are embryonic humans and foetal humans and neonatal humans and adolescent humans and adult humans and elderly humans and guess what? They're all human. The question we need to ask society is how should we treat embryonic humans?

What is the biblical way of thinking about embryos? The embryo is ultimately a mystery but if we can't be sure of its meaning or significance, what is an authentically Christian response to uncertainty? It seems to me, an authentic Christian response is to play safe. If you don't know whether there's a person there, then you play safe.

Contraception

What is a Christian view of contraception? This is quite controversial but my belief is that we don't intentionally destroy embryos and therefore using a means of contraception which will intentionally destroy embryos is wrong. My own belief therefore is that the morning after pill, designed to make sure that if there is an embryo it will fail to implant, is a deliberate attempt to create a very early abortion. However, the combined contraceptive pill works by preventing fertilisation, by preventing the sperm and the egg ever meeting. And I, like most Protestant Christians, believe there is a place in the context of a marriage where that kind of contraception is appropriate.

We can look at human beings either as Lego kits or as flawed masterpieces. This analogy came to me at a time when our house was completely full of Lego. A Lego kit has no intrinsic order. That's how many scientists think of the body; as a collection of kit and you can do amazing things with it. I want to suggest that a Christian way of thinking of the body is different – we think of the body as a wonderful masterpiece that has somehow been affected by the Fall. We can use technology to restore the masterpiece but what we mustn't do, just like art restorers, is to change the design. The original artist's design – God himself, the Creator – is normative. So there are still issues but it makes a difference between restorative treatment and enhancing treatment. Using technology to restore the masterpiece is appropriate. So, for instance, when we use *in vitro* fertilisation, are we using it to restore God's original plan? Are we using it to allow the unique love between a man and a woman to turn into a unique baby? Because if we are, then it could be argued we're restoring the masterpiece. Or are we using it to change the design completely, to change the relationship? So I think that IVF, using a married couple's sperm and egg to create a baby, maybe is part of a Christian response to infertility. There are still all sorts of issues about the technology. There are issues about the whole process, the way it's done and many Christians have decided they don't want to go that route.

The hard questions

What about when we have dilemmas, as we often do in the neonatal unit, where we're giving life support treatment and the question is, 'Are we doing the right thing for this baby?' This is where we balance the burdens and benefits of treatment. If treatment is bringing benefit, life and healing, then that's good. There are times when the burdens of treatment, of intensive care, can actually turn into a form of torture. In those situations, the Christian response is to say 'Enough.' Death can be both an evil which we fight against but also a strange kind of healing.

So we've learnt how to care for the dying baby. I think this is a wonderful Christian response. It's been one of the greatest privileges I've had, to care for dying babies over the years, to help babies to die well, at peace and in their mothers' arms.

I just want to tell you the story of Alan and Verity Mitchell. They were close friends of ours at All Souls Church and she became pregnant. It was their first pregnancy and they were overjoyed. Then the story turned to tragedy because they had the scans and it showed a terrible genetic condition called Edward syndrome which is universally lethal and has multiple malformations. In this situation, nearly everybody has an abortion.

After a great deal of heart-searching, Alan and Verity felt they couldn't do this. They had to carry on, this baby was still a gift from God. And after nine months, Christopher was born and he was a very small, placid but wonderful baby. He had this capacity to bring love out of other people and, to everyone's surprise, he didn't die immediately, he lived for a number of months. He was never able to grow. He was brought to church where he became almost like a little celebrity. Then after a number of months, little Christopher passed away and at his memorial service, there were over four hundred people. Because the truth was that, in some way, baby Christopher was a Godlike being, he reflected the character of the Lord Jesus himself. And it was a strange mystery. Sometimes we see God most clearly not in the powerful, not in the strong, not in the people who are the most impressive people. Where do we see God most clearly? We see him in the broken, bleeding body of a man on a cross. As one Christian put it: 'Christian love is a way of saying to another "It's good that you exist, it's good that you are in the world."'

What can you do?

Pray – we desperately need people to pray. Sometimes it's very lonely for those of us in the public arena. Sometimes we feel that the Christian Church doesn't understand why these issues are important and what impact they are having on our society. It's a spiritual battle:

behind all this political manoeuvring, there are forces of evil. Get informed; there are ways of getting informed.

Write to your MP; MPs respond when people write, if letters are short, well argued and from the heart. Support your Christian local crisis pregnancy centre. www.careconfidential.com is the group of Christian crisis pregnancy centres, and there is a lot more information and how to find your local centre available there. And the Christian Medical Fellowship website has a great deal of information – www.cmf.org.uk

Science at the end of life

Introduction

Death affects all of us. As I think about my death, I wonder whether I will die in peace, surrounded by people who love me? Will I die as a sudden event? Will I die in pain? If you go back to the Victorian era, they were so preoccupied with death that they lost the idea that Christ could bring resurrection. We've shifted the other way; our services so emphasise the fact that Christ brings new life, that we've lost the other side that to die well is a Christian duty. So one of the questions we have to ask ourselves is: what is a Christian way to die?

Statistics show that Britons are uniquely terrified by death. A poll carried out by *New Scientist* magazine found that 67 per cent of British people are 'petrified by the prospect of dying'. People are very worried that we're ageing as a population, and it fuels the question of euthanasia. Should we be mercy killing? How as a society are we going to cope with all these millions of elderly people? There is a big undercurrent wanting to push for the legalisation of euthanasia, and driving that demand is fear.

I had an interesting debate, some years ago, with Ludovic Kennedy, who was a great campaigner for euthanasia, and he said,

'I'm afraid of the process of dying.' People are afraid of dying and euthanasia seems like a quick fix.

What are people frightened of?

There are three things they are frightened of: and the first is fear of suffering terrible, uncontrollable pain. We've lost the idea that pain could have any positive value. To modern people, pain is utterly pointless. But it's not just fear of pain: palliative care is incredibly successful, when it's done skilfully, in controlling any pain. So the fears have moved on, and people are afraid of indignity, undignified dying. And above all, they're frightened of dependence. To secular people, dependence is the ultimate horror.

I've been involved in this debate for a number of years. Back in the nineties, there was a big push for euthanasia legislation and the whole debate was about pain, and the particular disease which people concentrated on was terminal cancer. In the last two years, there's been another big debate going on about euthanasia and it's changed. The debate is about dependence and the diseases have shifted. We're no longer talking about cancer, now we're talking about chronic degenerative disorders like motor neurone disease.

Our self respect comes from leading our own life, not being ushered along it by others, and one of the very powerful ideas is that my life is like a play. I'm the playwright and I'm writing my own script. So far it's been pretty good but now I'm coming to the last act and I'm terrified that the last act is going to ruin the whole thing: the play is going to end in drivelling idiocy and pain. I want to make sure that the last act fits with the rest of my life.

Social pressures

We're seeing a particular rise in chronic disability and degenerative conditions like Alzheimers. There are many other conditions where the brain and the central nervous system deteriorate and people end up in homes. The statistics are frightening and suggest approximately between one in five and one in ten of all of us are likely to be affected by one or other of these terminal degenerative conditions, unless something unusual happens, and so people worry about how we as a society are going to cope with the expense. People have plotted the health care costs and they find health care costs over a lifetime are very low, until towards the end when they rocket, and the health economists are worried about this.

Family breakup means that increasingly people are dying in isolation. The Western way of death is to shunt off our elderly, dependent people into homes and then to abandon them. Given the fact that families have broken up, is this the way we want to end? Surely euthanasia would be better than ending your life abandoned alone in a nursing home? So the push for euthanasia is not primarily about pain, the push is increasingly about control and about these social factors.

In most countries in the world euthanasia, intentional mercy killing, is illegal. It's covered in the UK under the Homicide Act. Doctors are no different from anybody else, we're covered by exactly the same law. But in a few countries in the world, euthanasia is legal and in one state – Oregon – in the USA, it's legal. Some statistics have been kept there, where people have been asked what reason they give for asking for physician-assisted suicide, and the most common reason that was given was controlling the time of death. Others include being ready to die; wanting to die at home instead of in hospital; existence being pointless; losing independence; poor quality of life – none of those talk about physical suffering. Somebody writing from the Oregon hospice association said: 'They are not using assisted suicide because they need it for the usual medical reasons. They are using it because they tend to be people who have always controlled the circumstances of their lives and they prefer to control their death in the same way.'

Changing the law

There's been a great movement, driven by Lord Joffe, to introduce euthanasia into the UK. and the Patient (Assisted Dying) Bill was introduced to the House of Lords. The Bill was intended to enable a competent adult, who was suffering unbearably as a result of a terminal or progressive physical illness, to receive medical help to die, at their own considered and persistent request. In order to actually be given lethal drugs, you had to be able to understand what was going on and you had to be likely to die within six months, and so, if you met all these criteria, then the doctors would give you a lethal concoction of drugs; you would take them and die.

There has been a lot of media spin about these issues. It is constantly said that doctors are doing euthanasia all the time, when they give drugs such as morphine, and this is already happening in hospices and so on. That is completely false. The drugs which are used in palliative care are completely different from the drugs used in euthanasia. The drugs used in euthanasia are all explicitly designed to kill and the intention in giving them is to cause death as instantaneously as possible.

Lord Joffe believes that this legislation is absolutely certain to happen in the UK. And because our law is so influential across the world, once the UK has legalised euthanasia then other countries will introduce euthanasia as well. We are incredibly influential internationally as a country, we're seen in many ways as a gold standard – heaven help us all – for legislation and for the regulation of medical and clinical issues.

The problems with euthanasia legislation

The fundamental issues

How do you argue against these things? In a public debate, arguing that the Bible says it's wrong to kill people isn't necessarily going to be helpful but there are other rational arguments that we can use. There is a fundamental logical problem in Lord Joffe's bill and in all euthanasia legislation that's been put forward. The problem is that the legislation says you have to have a combination of three things: unbearable suffering, being about to die and the competence to say 'I want to die.' But, logically, if unbearable suffering is moral justification for medical suicide, why do I have to have a terminal illness? Why do I have to be going to die in six months? What if I'm going to die in nine months but I'm in total agony? Would be immoral to kill me when I've got nine months to live but moral to kill me when I've got six months? What if I'm in such terrible agony, even if I'm not going to die? If unbearable suffering is justification for euthanasia then surely it should be justification, however long the patient is going to live. And if having a terminal illness is justification for being put out of my misery, then why do I have to be suffering? My life is pointless: I'm not actually in terrible pain, doctor, but I'm going to die, and I want to die now. So there are logical problems with this kind of legislation. And there are terrible risks: euthanasia legislation can go wrong.

A wrong diagnosis

People have this naïve belief that doctors always get it right and are totally reliable. If the doctor says I have x,y and z, then I must have x,y and z. The reality is that doctors get it wrong and if we get it wrong and we have polished you off with euthanasia, it's a bit difficult to do anything about it.

The wrong prognosis

If a doctor says, 'I think you've got three months to live' the one thing you can guarantee is that you're not going to live for three months. You might live for three days or three years but it's exceedingly unlikely that you'll live for three months. Medical prognostication is incredibly unreliable. Nearly always, whenever I've confidently predicted when a patient is going to die, I've got it resoundingly wrong. We just can't predict when people are going to die, and therefore the idea that doctors can confidently say this person is going to die in six months is just wrong.

The possibilities for abuse

I'm not going to go through them in detail but there are the possibilities of abuse by health professionals and relatives, the increased anxieties for the elderly and the unwanted and also the effect of killing on doctors. What are you doing to human beings once they've broken this final taboo? And what are we doing in society when the taboo side is being rehabilitated as a noble and an honourable way to die?

The history of the Bill

In 2006, much to Lord Joffe's amazement, there was a collaboration between Christian people, people from other faith groups, palliative care doctors and disabilities rights groups. They got together and had a united, effective campaign against this euthanasia legislation and the legislation wasn't passed. So they've gone away to plan how to reintroduce the legislation. This is going to come back repeatedly in our lifetime and humanly speaking, sooner or later, the legislation will be passed unless we as Christian people resist it and God has mercy on our nation. It looks like the next assault is going to come in Scotland and the strategy now is if we can get it done through the Scottish parliament, then it will become like a Trojan horse and spread to the rest of the country.

Euthanasia by stealth

We are not only up against this full frontal approach to have mercy killing legalised. It's also euthanasia by stealth or neglect and this is already going on in our hospitals. Some health care staff are deliberately withholding food and fluids from patients who are admitted to hospital who are acutely ill, who might be unconscious from a stroke, maybe just elderly, who may be demented and so on. Sometimes the intention is to kill people who are felt to be worthless and withholding food and fluid is a hundred per cent effective way of ending someone's life.

I know some people with chronic disabilities, in wheelchairs, and they've said to me 'I'm terrified of having a chest infection and being admitted to hospital because I don't think I'm going to come out. Somebody will decide I'm a burden and will allow me to die.' Isn't that terrible? That a hospital, which should be a place of safety, can become a place where someone's going to decide your life isn't worth living. I'm afraid that's a fear that elderly or disabled people express.

The Mental Capacity Act

This is one of the very important ways in which the law has changed and something that doctors and other health care professionals are trying to think our way through. I suspect most people haven't realised that this has happened but it's a big change in the law on health care, particularly at the end of life. Under the old law, ultimately you had the right to choose your own treatment and what kind of treatment you had. If you became incapacitated then the doctor had to act in your best interests, and although the doctor would talk to relatives, ultimately and legally, it was the doctor's responsibility to decide what was in the patient's best interest. By and large, that system has worked for hundreds if not thousands of years, reasonably well. Sometimes there'd be problems, there's always been the possibility of rogue doctors but, by and large, people have been prepared to trust doctors to make wise decisions.

In the new age, we don't trust anybody and we don't trust doctors any more than we trust other people. The new law is designed to allow us, the individual, to decide how we want to die: what kind of treatment we have. We want to make sure that we have control. But how do you retain control if you've lost awareness, become confused or are unconscious? The law has suggested two fundamental ways that you retain control.

Living wills

You write down, in advance, detailed instructions about what you want to happen to you, an advanced statement. The Mental Capacity Act says that, provided it's written down in the proper way, this advanced statement is now legally binding. It forces the doctors to act according to what you said. If you have said, 'If I become unconscious, I do not wish any machine to keep me alive' and it's properly witnessed and signed and there are various criteria and so on, then if you're knocked down in the street and you're brought into a hospital unconscious and this living will is found and brought to the hospital, the doctors are legally forced to follow what you've written. Even if you changed your mind in the meantime, even if you said 'I wasn't talking about being knocked down in the street,' if that's what it says, that's what we have to do. The government is saying that all of us should be writing down how we want to die, what we want to happen to us, whether we want to be resuscitated, what happens to us if we get dementia and so on.

Power of attorney

There's another possibility that the law says: instead of writing down what we want, we nominate a person and hand over to them the authority to make decisions on our behalf. And the decisions they make on our behalf will be legally binding. So I nominate my wife as the lasting power of attorney and then I develop some terrible problem and I'm on a life support system. The doctors say, 'What are we going to do?' and my wife is going to take full legal responsibility. If she says, 'I think the right thing to do is to switch off the machinery' then they will say 'OK.' Or if she says, 'I think you should carry on' they'll say 'OK.'

So instead of a doctor taking that responsibility, now somebody who's never been in this situation before is suddenly going to have to take full legal responsibility and live for the rest of their life with the consequences of the decision. Do you want to put that burden on to your wife? Or one of your relatives? Who would you trust to take that decision? Who would it be fair to ask to carry that burden of responsibility? As Christian doctors, we are trying to work out what's a Christian response to this. What we probably need to do is to write some Christian examples of advanced statements that talk about a Christian faith and a hope. It's something I've done for elderly Christian people who've asked me for help and it's still something we're trying to learn about.

What is the Christian response?

This is the world in which we live, how on earth are we going to think about it? Before the Christian era, when the Hippocratic oath first came into existence, both physician-assisted suicide and euthanasia were explicitly stated in it. It says 'I will use treatment to help the sick according to my ability and judgement but I will never use it to injure or wrong them. I will never give a poison to my patient, even if asked and neither will I suggest such a plan.' Euthanasia and physician-assisted suicide are not new ideas, they've been there for thousands of years. Right from the beginning, Hippocratic doctors said, 'We will never use our skill to injure or harm.' That is a tradition which is now being threatened: doctors are being asked to become killers.

Biblical ethics, the way we treat one another, comes from biblical anthropology, the way we're made. A human life is not just a gift of God's grace, it's also a reflection of his person. We find at the beginning, in Genesis 9:6, this taboo against the shedding of blood: 'Whoever sheds the blood of man. by man shall his blood be shed.' Why? Because God has made man in his own image. This verse links the ancient taboo against the shedding of blood with the image of God. In Christian thinking, the destruction of an innocent human life is always wrong, because it is a profound insult to the being and character of God himself.

We are not isolated autonomous individuals. God has made us locked into a family: all of us have fathers, mothers, relatives, friends and dependants. We are locked together in mutual bonds of dependence and therefore, if you hurt yourself, it damages me. If you don't treat yourself with respect then you're saying something about me and if I damage myself, I'm doing something to you. We're all locked together in bonds; and although suicide is often a desperate act of people driven mad by despair, we know how damaging suicide is to those who survive, how often it leaves deep sadness.

What about martyrdom? Didn't Jesus commit suicide on the cross? Isn't there such a thing as a noble suicide? No – those are two quite different things. Suicide destroy your life because there's nothing worth living for, martyrdom is to give your life because there's something worth dying for. It's all to do with the intention. What am I giving my life for? Jesus went to the cross not out of despair: his intention was to give his life for others, as the supreme example of altruism.

Dependence: part of God's plan

People are terrified of dependence and this is the message we need to send out to the modern world. Dependence is not an alien, subhuman, undignified condition: it's part of God's plan for our lives. If Jesus, as a baby, was totally dependent on the love of others, then it's good enough for us. If we have to have our bottoms wiped, to be winded, to be fed by a teaspoon, it doesn't mean that our fundamental value, our fundamental significance, our fundamental Godlikeness is in any way impaired.

But, as we saw in the first lecture, the suffering is not something we can obliterate. It's a mystery which demands presence. When we see people who are suffering, the first human response is to withdraw, because it's unpleasant. But in fact that's terribly damaging; we send a signal of rejection. The Christlike response is to share the pain. Suffering is a call to come alongside, to be there, not with any quick solution, not with any neat answers: just to be there.

Palliative care has been developed as a wonderful Christian response to the problem of suffering. If you go back to the sixties, Christian doctors were confronted with the terrible dilemma: on the one hand, you could watch people dying of cancer in terrible agony or you could kill them, to put them out of their misery. A few Christian pioneers said, 'We are not going to do evil.' If you're confronted with two evil possibilities what do you do? Answer: you do neither of them, you create a new way. They created the whole new speciality of palliative care, as a response to the statement 'There's nothing more that we can do.' This is never true, there is always more that we can do. Palliative care deals with total pain, not just physical pain: it's psychological, relational and spiritual pain. But the problem is that expert palliative care isn't widely available. Many people die without proper palliative care and I think that's a scandal but I think it's also a call, if you're a carer, a way in which you can use your skills. There are many ways that you could be the hands of Christ to the dying in this way.

Good medicine needs to know its limits, it needs to know when it should struggle against death and evil but also when it has to say enough is enough and when death changes from being an enemy to being a gateway to a new existence, even a strange form of healing. Sometimes we need to say to our medical attendants enough is enough, it's time to go, it's time we recognised that death can be a kind of healing.

What is a good death?

From a secular perspective, a good death is one which occurs at the time and manner I choose, my dignity depends on the fact that I'm not dependent on others, I want to die without suffering as a free and independent person. From a Christian perspective, a good death is one where my pain and symptoms are controlled, where I'm surrounded by people who love me and care for me. A good death is an opportunity to concentrate on the most important things in life and look towards an eternal hope which transcends the grave. In the medieval ages, people's greatest fear was a quick death – you'd never be able to prepare yourself to meet your Maker. What a terrible thing to be catapulted into eternity and never prepare yourself for death. Nowadays, modern people say 'That's the way to go, bang! Never knew what hit him.' Is that a good death? I think the opportunity to prepare to say goodbye, to heal, to grow – that's the way God meant us to die.

Caring for those with dementia

The important thing to realise is that there's been massive advances taking place over the last two or three years of ways of caring for people with dementia. If you can get the best expert help, there are all sorts of positive advances, better way of establishing communication, of finding ways of relating and helping people and there may be new drugs coming as well which are going to help and advance the care of dementia. It isn't a completely black future but get skilled professional help, share the burden and the privilege. Sometimes caring is a fantastic privilege. I've been a carer for most of my life and it's one of the great, fantastic privileges that God has given me, to be the hands of Christ. If you're caring for someone, share the privilege, bring other people to share that privilege, including young people. Young people can grow from being involved in caring. It's part of our family life together, it's part of bearing one another's burdens and fulfilling the law of Christ. Fight for adequate resources. Use every route for establishing and maintaining communication. Care for the whole person, including spiritual care.

A friend of mine told me a story. She was caring for her mother with advanced dementia, a lady who'd had a great spiritual life but now had become almost completely mute, unable to communicate. And even though her mother couldn't respond, she was talking about prayer, how she was praying for her and other people. Then, amazingly, her mother suddenly said, 'I pray too.' And this woman said, 'What do you say to God?' And she said, 'I . . . say . . . hello.' That was it. Yet somewhere, in there, the person is still there.

We must care for people, not only in the light of what they once were. Christianity is always hope filled, looking to the future, and we care for people in the light of what, by God's grace, they may become. The dawn is rising and it's going to come, it's going to grow into the full light of day. That's the way God planned it, that's the way God wanted it to be. May we live in the light of that coming dawn to his glory.

The Addresses

Standing firm:
1 Thessalonians 3:1–13

by Jonathan Lamb

Jonathan Lamb

Jonathan is presently Director of Langham Preaching for Langham Partnership International, a global programme seeking to encourage a new generation of preachers and teachers. This is a ministry which networks with national leaders in many parts of the world, including Africa, Asia and Latin America, as well as Central Europe and Eurasia. Formerly a chairman of the Keswick Convention and of Word Alive, Jonathan still serves as a trustee for Keswick, and is a regular speaker at 'Keswicks' in other countries. He is a member of the preaching team in his local church, St Andrew's in Oxford. He is married to Margaret and they have three daughters.

Standing firm: 1 Thessalonians 3:1–13

A few days ago I had the opportunity to meet some young Christians from Cambodia. They had recently taken leadership in their church in Phnom Penh. You might remember that Cambodia emerged from the intense suffering of the 1970s with a shattered economy and a very vulnerable church. But in the last few years there has been remarkable church growth – there are now over 250,000 believers. The men I met were taking up leadership in the church, and they told me that it had taken ten years for the church to be established and for nationals now to take leadership. Ten years of work – in pioneer evangelism, in church planting, in teaching and training, and finally in appointing leaders. And they compared this to the missionary activity of Korean believers in the country: they try to do the job in three years! It's close to impossible, they said.

What about the church in Thessalonica? Paul had been there for just three weeks! What chance would such a church have of being established, let alone maturing? The first Christians in all of Europe – but what hope of survival? And given the pressures which this little Christian community was under, how could it possibly remain steady? Paul's concern for the well-being of this church is graphically expressed in our passage, 1 Thessalonians 3. Would they stand firm?

It is very relevant for us. Can the Church around the world stand firm against wind and tide? How can the church in Zimbabwe keep the faith? How can the small minority of three thousand evangelicals in Turkey cope with the opposition? How can the church in Islamic republics stand firm? And can you and I stand firm against the growing pressure which we Christians face – the temptations of living in a secular society, the challenges of swimming against the tide, the pressure of standing up for Jesus in a plural context where Jesus is denied? The Thessalonians faced all kinds of pressures, as we shall see. But notice the key verse 8: 'For now we really live, since you are standing firm in the Lord.'

Paul had been deeply concerned about them, so much so that their fate placed a question mark over his mission – would it prove to be a failure? 'Have our efforts been useless?' (v5). He was so concerned that when he eventually receives news from Timothy that all was well, he was overjoyed. 'But Timothy has just now come to us from you and has brought good news about your faith and love' (v6) – he uses the word for preach the gospel, because it was such good news! They were standing firm – the word is not the usual one, but it is a word which includes the idea of stability, firmness and steadfastness. They were rock solid!

It's important to note the whole phrase – 'standing firm *in the Lord*'. These Thessalonians sustained their steadfast commitment by being in close union with the Lord. He was the rock on which they stood, the one who strengthened their resolve to live with faith and love. So in turning to this chapter, there are several important encouragements to us to stand firm.

1. Pressure is inevitable

Encouragement to stand firm? Really? Pressure is inevitable? Yes, Paul is implying, because knowing about these pressures – and realising what they are about – helps you to remain steadfast. There are two ways in which the passage tells us these pressures will manifest themselves.

First, they could be distracted by trials: Paul says in verse 3 he sent Timothy 'so that no one would be unsettled by these trials'. The pressures facing these young Christians could really shake up their faith. The word is used in the New Testament for trials, persecution, suffering and trouble of all kinds. And it was not so much the fact of trials but the intensity of these trials that so concerned Paul.

The second way in which these pressures were exerted was this: they could be disturbed by Satan. 'I was afraid that in some way the tempter might have tempted you and our efforts might have been useless' (v5). We see the same at the end of chapter 2: 'I wanted to come and see you again – but Satan thwarted us' (v18). Satan is spoken of in every part of the New Testament, tempting Jesus, tempting his disciples, hindering missionaries like Paul. But the interesting thing to notice is how Paul talks about these pressures. Look what he says in verse 3. 'You know quite well that we were destined for them. In fact, when we were with you, we kept telling you that we would be persecuted. And it turned out that way, as you well know'. In fact, Calvin wrote that it was almost as if God had said 'you are Christians on this condition – you will suffer . . .'

And the verse implies something more. It is not just a matter of chance or blind fate: the emphasis of verse 3 is that this is something within God's purpose. You are destined or appointed for these trials. Mysterious as it might seem, God's hand is in this. Do you remember how Paul saw his thorn in the flesh? It was both a messenger of Satan, he said, but also something which God had in some sense given him, and which God was going to use for particular purposes. So whatever the source of the hardships – the work of Satan, or hostile opposition – we can hold on to the truth that we are never beyond God's sovereign care, the situation is never out of control. Whether we are a struggling church, or a wavering Christian – distracted by trials or disturbed by Satan – we hold to the truth, to the rock solid certainties of God's good purposes and fatherly care. Standing firm *in the Lord.*

So first, pressures are inevitable: they are part of living out the Christian life. It is a sign that we really are on God's side. Properly understood, the experience of pressure strengthens not weakens our commitment to stand firm in the Lord.

2. Friends are vital

We have seen each evening that Paul was deeply concerned for the
Thessalonians. He not only preached the gospel, he shared his own
life – he loved, encouraged, supported, prayed. Even when his own
life was in danger, or even when he was isolated, his first thought was
the young church. He was so concerned about them, he sent
Timothy. Paul and Silas had already been in trouble in Thessalonica,
so Timothy was best placed to slip over the border unrecognised. But
it was costly for Paul. He was in Athens, about to face the philosophers and idolators, and perhaps he would once again encounter a
hostile reaction. But he writes, 'When we could stand it no longer,
we thought it best to be left by ourselves' (v1). It's a strong word
which can be used of being abandoned or even of dying.

But his concern for his friends meant he would send one of his
closest friends and fellow workers – the very person who could
have supported him in a new and challenging mission. Well, he
would tackle that on his own, because what really mattered was the
well-being of the small church in Thessalonica. And look how he
describes Timothy's ministry in verse 2: 'We sent Timothy to
strengthen and encourage you in the faith'. He did two things, and
both are to do with establishing. The word 'strengthen' is a word
from the building trade; it means to 'buttress'. Timothy's job was to
build them up. It is never enough for us just to sign up to be a
Christian: our calling is to grow up, to become mature, steady,
standing firm. In fact the word 'strengthen' is often used for the
nurture of Christians, and this strengthening and nurturing is a
vital part of church life and growth. It is needed for young
Christians who are facing many new challenges; and it is needed
by older Christians who are in danger of becoming spiritually stag-
nant.

And the second word in verse 2 is 'encourage', which has the
sense of being called alongside someone to strengthen and exhort
them. So Timothy would have strengthened them in the faith, urg-
ing them to hold on to the apostolic teaching. More than that, we
see in verse 10 that although they were standing firm, growing in

faith and love, there was more to be done. Paul wanted to get back to see them again 'and supply what is lacking in your faith'. Here Paul uses a word that is used of mending nets in Mark 1, and of equipping Christians for the work of ministry in Ephesians 4. So he wanted to make good the deficiencies, to restore and equip them for full maturity.

In both ways then – Paul's generosity and Timothy's ministry – here is an example of how to care for those who are under pressure, how to encourage Christians to stand firm. And we urgently need to do the same. How is it in your church? Some of us here are Christian leaders – pastors, house group leaders, youth leaders, small group leaders . . . Whatever our responsibility, our job is to give this kind of energetic, costly support and encouragement. Facing all kinds of pressures, friends are vital. We need to be roped together. In fact, in verse 8 when Paul heard the good news, he said: 'For now we really live, since you are standing firm in the Lord'. Now we're living! In other words, his life was completely bound up with theirs. 'My heart is beating, the blood is coursing through my veins, when you stand firm. This is what really matters for me.' So in verses 9 and 10 he can't express his thanks to God sufficiently strongly, he is so overjoyed. That is what Christian fellowship is all about. I feel the pressures that others are facing. And under pressure myself, I need the encouragement of others who will remind me of the promises of God's word, provoke my faith in the Lord, insert vertebra in my elastic spine, encourage me by being alongside in the trials.

Do you know whose ministry we need more of in our churches? It's Barnabas. The church sent him to Antioch and 'when he arrived and saw the evidence of the grace of God, he was glad and encouraged them to remain true to the Lord with all their hearts' (Acts 11:23). Friends who strengthen and encourage are friends who urge us to keep to the firm foundations of the gospel, to remember that we are not beyond the Spirit's comforting presence and the Father's compassionate care. That's a job for all us. Let's keep saying to one another: stick to it, remain true to the Lord, persevere, stand firm.

3. Prayer is essential

In verses 10 to 13 Paul moves to prayer. We will come to the content in a moment. But let me make two quick observations. First, it is committed prayer: it is one of the ways in which his affectionate concern for them is expressed, and there is a remarkable solidarity here. He states in verse 10 that 'night and day we pray most earnestly'. In chapter 2 verse 9 he has already said that he works 'night and day' so as not to be a burden to them, so how are we to understand this? I wonder if you have had this experience. Maybe a close friend or relative is having a serious operation; or your child is in the middle of an important exam or a job interview. You know the feeling: you can't wait for news of how it has gone. And as you wait, every few minutes it surfaces in your mind again, and you pray for them. I do this because I am so concerned about the situation, so concerned about their welfare that it naturally springs to mind, maybe every few minutes in the midst of many other things. That's exactly how it should be as we pray for one another. Fellow Christians under pressure need us to bring their situation to God.

Email can be a curse but it is also a blessing. In our home we receive many prayer requests that way, updating us on situations in other countries, or on friends who are facing trials, or illness or Satanic attack. And we try to take them seriously – to pray when the email drops into the in-box, and to send a short message of encouragement back. Prayer is deflecting all of our situations God-ward. I like the illustration that Alec Motyer uses: Christians are like mirrors, angled so that whatever meets us on our journey, we immediately deflect it to God, send it up to our heavenly Father. Such praying helps us see our problems in the proper perspective.

This links to the second important thing. It is God-centred prayer: verses 10–13 are full of God's work, heralding what God can do. Think about the prayers in our prayer meetings. Many of them are 'O Lord, we ask for . . .' Whereas the great Bible prayers are different. They are not 'O Lord, *we* . . .' but 'O Lord, *you* . . .' Do you remember the early Christian prayer in Acts 4, when the small church was under pressure? How did they pray? 'Sovereign Lord –

you . . . You made the heavens and the earth and the sea, and every-thing in them . . .'

Do you sometimes feel overwhelmed by the struggle to live the Christian life? Do you feel it's impossible to overcome the pull of one sin or another, or to live with integrity in a home or a job where everyone else is going in the opposite direction to you? Do you feel the issues you are coping with in terms of your service for God, or your relationships, or your future, seem to be way beyond your control? For the pressures we are facing – distracted by trials and disturbed by Satan – we urgently need to depend on God's mighty power. Paul's emphasis in Ephesians 6:10 is important for us every day: 'Be strong in the Lord and in his mighty power.' Perhaps it would be better to say, not 'be strong' but 'be strengthened', receive his strength, and then you will be strong. In verse 10 he uses three different words: power, might, strength. And he uses the same trio of words in Ephesians 1 when he describes Jesus' resurrection: 'this power is like the working of his mighty strength which he exerted in Christ when he raised him from the dead'. God's power which overcomes death, which elevated Jesus far above all rule and authority, is the same power which is at work in us. It is the resource we need and for which we must pray. That leads us to the final encouragement:

4. God is unstoppable

The prayer in verses 11 to 13 makes the point: it is ultimately God's work.

First, verse 11, **God directs**: 'Now may our God and Father himself and our Lord Jesus clear the way for us to come to you.' And sure enough, God answered, and Paul was able to visit them again on his way back to Jerusalem. Satan might hinder, but ultimately God's purposes are unstoppable.

Second, verse 12, **God equips**: 'May the Lord make your love increase and overflow for each other and for everyone else, just as ours does for you.' Our spiritual growth is in God's hands too. And this is a partnership. So on the one hand, Paul sees it as God's work: 'the Lord make your love increase' (3:12). But then in the next chapter: 'You love all the brothers – we urge you to do so more and more' (4:10). There is a God-centredness, but that stimulates not lessens our sense of responsibility. We co-operate with God to activate his purposes in our lives.

And third, verse 13, **God completes**: 'May he strengthen your hearts so that you will be blameless and holy in the presence of our God and Father when our Lord Jesus comes with all his holy ones.' God completes what he has begun. It is unstoppable. 'Blameless' implies unblameable. On that future day when Jesus returns, nothing will stand against us, no more of Satan's accusations can harm us. And as always, that future anticipation of Christ's return is a key stimulus for us. There's no greater encouragement to live the life of faith and love and hope, to live in holiness, to stand firm – than the prospect of Christ's return. Fixing our eyes on Jesus, the coming King, sets all of our trials and Satanic pressures in perspective.

God is unstoppable! I hope you feel the force of this passage with its strong encouragements to stand firm. Around the world Christians are a small minority; young churches live under oppressive governments; Christians like us feel our frailty and vulnerability. How can we be strengthened so that Satan does not disturb us and trials don't distract us?

First, we need to be realistic about our Christian calling and thankful for God's purposes in suffering – *pressure is inevitable*. Second, *friends are vital* – people who support us and people whom we support, who encourage us to stand on the gospel foundations. Third, *prayer is essential*: to bring to the Lord day by day and hour by hour our own needs and those of others in the family of God. But most of all – we need the conviction that *God is unstoppable*. God completes the work which he has begun.

Last week I also met believers from Myanmar. They told me of the terrible devastation to the country and the unbelievable suffering of their people following the cyclone. And one pastor told me of a man he had visited, who was caught in the floods and the winds with his children. He was distraught because he had to hold on to a tree, whilst also holding on to one of his children. One other child was holding on to his neck, but was washed away. But the child whom he held, survived. And after all we have said about standing firm, this is the ultimate reality: it is not our hold of God that matters, but his hold upon us. Underneath are the everlasting arms; as Jesus said about his sheep, no-one can snatch them out of the Father's hand. When it comes to standing firm, as Hudson Taylor expressed it: 'It is not so much great faith we need, as faith in a great God.'

Living to please God:
1 Thessalonians 4:1–12

by Oscar Miriu

Oscar Miriu

Oscar Miriu dedicated his life to Christ in 1983, and has served as the Senior Pastor of the Nairobi Chapel since 1991. In that time, he has seen the church grow from twenty people to over three thousand, with nineteen church plants. His personal mission is to raise up a legacy of African leaders for the Church of Christ worldwide. He holds a B.Sc (Zoology) from the University of Delhi in India, and a M.Div from the Nairobi Evangelical Graduate School of Theology. Pastor Oscar and his wife Bea have four daughters.

Living to please God:
1 Thessalonians 4:1–12

Introduction

In the book of Thessalonians, the beginning of this chapter marks a watershed. This is when Paul seems to say, 'Having spoken about those things that concerned me in chapters 1, 2 and 3, and my visit to you, now let me turn aside and deal with those things that concern you.' He turns aside from his apology about his time in Thessalonica to dealing with morals that concern the Thessalonians. He almost seems to say 'Enough about me, now let's focus on you.'

Apostolic authority (vs 1–2)

He begins by asserting his apostolic authority. He says, 'we ask you' – very gracious, very kind words – then goes on to say, 'we urge you in the name of the Lord Jesus'. He almost seems to say, 'but, just in case you didn't understand, I am speaking by the authority given me by the Lord Jesus Christ.' You can tell that Paul is about to launch into a very important statement and to reinforce this (v2) he reminds them, 'you know the instructions'. Some of your translations don't use the word 'instructions', it says 'commands'. The word that they're translating 'instructions' or 'commands' is not often used. It's a strong word that was used by a military commander telling his troops what they are to do or by a judge in giving a ruling. It basically means 'This is a non-negotiable. ' So what is Paul about to launch into?

Sexual purity (vs 3-8)

'It is God's will that you should be sanctified': set apart, like those special vessels that are put aside in the glass cabinet in the dining room and only used for very special guests. This is Paul's call, in the strongest possible terms, that we must avoid sexual immorality. These are strong words and Paul makes no apology for them because, as he says, these are not the words of men but the words of God himself.

Why would Paul talk to the Thessalonians in such strong terms? One of the reasons could be that Paul, who was writing from the city of Corinth, was looking around him and he was worried for his brothers and sisters in Thessalonica. Corinth housed the temple of the Greek god Aphrodite and it was a town where licentiousness ruled. Every night the thousand prophetesses would come down from their mountain temple into the city to prostitute and sell their wares. Paul sees this and his heart is gripped with fear for his fellow believers.

One of the Greek historians, a person from this place, says, 'We keep prostitutes for pleasure, we keep mistresses for the day-to-day needs of the body, we keep wives for the begetting of children and for the faithful guardianship of our homes.' There seems to have been no sense of shame about extra-marital affairs and the Romans were no different. They lived with the same seeking after pleasure, with no apology.

Is it any different today? I am dismayed in my own context and, as I have travelled around the world, by the numbers of people, even Christians, who are living in total disregard to what Paul tells us in 1 Thessalonians 4:1-8. Young people seem to presume that it's okay to sleep around, young couples believe 'Because we have made a promise of marriage to one another, it's okay for us to sleep together.' Married men and women cheat on one another. If you are in an affair, you have defiled yourself and the name of God. Paul makes no apology for speaking in such strong terms. If you're sleeping around, this does not please God. If you have fed your lust, the words of the Lord to us are 'The Lord will punish men for all such sins, as we have already told you and warned you. For God did not call us to be impure, but to live a holy life.'

Paul isn't just saying 'live a life of purity.' In fact, twice in this passage, Paul uses the words 'more and more.' He's telling us to live a life of purity, but live it more and more. And this applies to all of us. None of us will ever reach a place where we'll say, 'I have arrived. I no longer need to be concerned about this matter because I have reached the topmost level that one can arrive to.'

My thinking was helped when I read this analogy, that spiritual fitness is like physical fitness. It's no good to say, 'I used to be in the Royal Air Force and boy, we could run ten kilometres in twenty minutes. We were fit.' That was years ago! That has almost no bearing on where you are today. The one who remains physically fit is the one who gets up every morning and goes out for a run or a walk. The same is true with spiritual fitness and maturity. The fact that I attended Bible school thirty years ago has nothing to do with today. The mature one is the one who gets up, takes up the word and reads it on a daily basis and, day by day, more and more, seeks spiritual fitness. Then they remain fit.

When I was in college, I did a number of classes on pastoral counselling and one of the things that our teacher taught us is that when you're counselling, you never show a sense of shock when somebody reveals something that is surprising. I was a young pastor and had only been at the church for a year or two, and a lady came to see me. She was in a very difficult marriage and she wanted to share about this. I'm trying to do everything right and so I'm attending and she's baring her heart and talking. And, as we're talking together and I'm listening attentively and trying to figure out how to encourage her, all of a sudden she seemed to veer off in the conversation. She said, 'Pastor, I find you very attractive.' I'm sitting there trying not to show any shock at where this conversation is going, keeping a straight face, and she says, 'I think I have fallen in love with you.' And I'm thinking,

'Oh dear, this conversation's going in the wrong direction.' But I was young, I didn't know how to do these things, I'm trying not to show my shock and I asked her, 'How long have you been feeling this way?'

I think my brain was a little slow! After that conversation, I made a couple of decisions. I realised this could be a continuing problem and I need to set some standards. Standard number one is 'Always discuss these sorts of situations with my wife.' And I made a couple of other decisions. One is that even my office is too compromising a situation. I made another commitment, I said 'I will not counsel more than two, maybe three times at the most, with a single lady in this sort of setting. As quickly as possible, I need to transfer these sort of counselling situations to the same gender so that I can protect myself.' I have gone on to make other decisions: I will not take a lady out for an appointment to a restaurant.

The question I should ask all of us is 'How have your battles for purity been different this year, compared with last year? How have you grown? How are you working to get to the next level of purity?' Billy Graham, the great evangelist says that it's not the first look; it's a second look that is a sin. I have set standards for myself concerning these things, standards that I battle with constantly. I want high standards because I want to live in a way that is pleasing to my Lord. My standards are unapologetically high and it's not about legalism, rules that I impose on other people. These are my standards that I may honour my Lord because I want to live a life that is pleasing to him.

I constantly remind myself of these words in Psalm 16:5, where the Psalmist says, 'LORD, you have assigned me my portion and my cup; you have made my lot secure. The boundary lines have fallen for me in pleasant places; surely I have a delightful inheritance.' The boundaries that God has put around me for sexual purity are good boundaries, they have fallen in pleasant places and whether I am single or married. I will not fight them. I will not cross over them. Instead I will live within the confines of the boundaries he has set, rejoicing in the space that he has given me, whether single or married.

After finishing my degree, I came to Kenya, where women did not dress modestly and these were the days of chiffon. I wasn't a

Christian then and I didn't have the standards that I seek to uphold today and so I'm walking through Nairobi and my eyes are like saucers. I fine-tuned the art of undressing women as I passed them and this became like bondage to me, an art I participated in at every opportunity. Not long after that that I came to know Christ as my Lord and Saviour and I realised I had a problem. I had done this so long that it was something I did without even thinking about. I prayed 'Lord, please give me victory over this.' Then I read a story of a missionary who had struggled with the same problem and finally he said, 'Lord, every time I give in to this urge to undress women this way, I will pray for a missionary brother or sister somewhere around the world.' And, as you can imagine, he was constantly praying. He became such a prayer warrior for the work of missions around the world, as a result of this, that it seemed that Satan stopped of necessity tempting him because he was praying so much against the work of Satan. This little story gave me encouragement and I covenanted to do the same. In time, God enabled me to have victory over this.

Where are your battles? And this isn't just a battle for the young ones. It amazes me that Job is an elderly man, a grandfather when we meet him in the early chapters of Job, yet in chapter 31:1, Job says, 'I made a covenant with my eyes not to look lustfully at a girl.' It's not just for the young, it's for all of us.

Brotherly love (vs 9-12)

How are you growing when it comes to your love for fellow brothers and sisters in Christ?

Being a student in India was very difficult. These were the days when many people in the internal parts of India had not met Africans and wherever we went, we always had children following us, pointing at us and calling us all sorts of names. In the Hindu pantheon of gods, the evil ones are always black and so they had names for us that associated us with evil. Many times, they would say that we were a people without a soul and had been cursed therefore to be black.

I remember one day, having left college early in the afternoon, going home to the estate where I'd rented a little room. The children were on holiday and they were out playing on the streets and as I walked down towards the place where I stayed, the children quickly stopped their games and dashed into their gated compounds to get out of my way, because they were afraid of me. And one little child went up to their gate and the gate was locked. This child clung on to those gates and screamed for help, terrified that I was coming down towards her.

That little incident and picture tore my heart apart. I went back to my room and I cursed myself for my colour. 'What is wrong with me? How can a child who is so young, maybe just three or four years old, be so terrified by me? Am I not human?' I began to hate my Indian hosts with a passion because of this. But when I came to accept Christ as my Lord and Saviour and to realise the awesome truth that Jesus Christ loved and died for them as much as he did me, I recognised that I could not afford to hate them while calling on the name of the Lord as my Saviour. And I made a covenant as a young Christian then that I would seek with all my heart to treat all men equally, because Christ died for them. My prayer became, 'Lord, forgive them for they do not know what they do when they point at me. Help me to love them nevertheless because you loved them enough to die for them.'

It's been a joy for my wife and I to be here among you and to see how gracious, warm, inviting and welcoming you all have been. My colour doesn't matter, I am loved and received as one who has been loved by the Lord. I cheer the Lord for that, that he has touched your heart in this way. Is this true all around in your life?

This concept that we are on an upward journey, seeking as Christians in multiple areas of discipline to grow in our love for the Lord, extends beyond these two areas that Paul writes to the Thessalonians about. One of my favourite passages is 2 Corinthians 8:7 where Paul talks about five areas that he encourages the Corinthians to excel in: 'But just as you excel in everything – in faith, in speech, in knowledge, in complete earnestness and in your love for us – see that you also excel in this grace of giving.' In other words, the expectation is that, in your faith, you are pursuing excellence; in the way you talk, you are seeking to excel, to speak only words that encourage others and build them up. In your knowledge and your pursuit of understanding of the things of God, it's not good enough that you were reading a certain sort of book last week, go to the next level, start reading to understand even more that you may excel and that you may grow in your earnestness and passion for the Lord. Seek to excel in your giving, so that this year you are giving more generously with a heart that overflows even more than you did last year.

I know that both these areas are an area of tension and battle for so many. There may be those of us who in God's grace have fought this battle long and have honoured the Lord in it. As we come to the end of our time together, I want to call on young men and older men, single men and married men, young women and older women, single women and married. Paul's plea is for all of us and we need to put our stake in the ground and say 'Lord, I want to go further and to pursue more and more the purity of a sanctified life.'

Back to the future:
1 Thessalonians 4:13 – 5:11

by Dr John Lennox

Dr John Lennox

John Lennox is a Professor of Mathematics at Oxford University, Fellow in Mathematics and the Philosophy of Science, and Pastoral Advisor at Green College, Oxford. He lectures on Science and Religion in the University of Oxford and teaches at the Oxford Centre for Christian Apologetics. He is the author of *God's undertaker – has science buried God?* He has lectured extensively in N. America, Eastern and Western Europe on mathematics, the philosophy of science, Christian apologetics and the exposition of Scripture. He has debated with Richard Dawkins on 'The God Delusion' both in the US and the UK, and with Christopher Hitchens in Edinburgh. His hobbies are languages, amateur astronomy, bird–watching and some walking. John is married to Sally, and they have three grown-up children and four grandchildren, and live near Oxford.

Back to the future:
1 Thessalonians 4:13 – 5:11

History is moving towards a goal; every chapter of this book ends with a comment on the coming of the Lord Jesus. And at the very beginning of the book, Paul reminds the Thessalonians that the second coming of Christ is an integral part of the Christian message. He describes their conversion as a turning to God from idols, to serve the living and the true God and to wait for his Son from heaven. And those two dimensions of time – serving in the present and waiting – belong together because the present and the future are inextricable.

A little bit of logical thought will show you that none of us can live for the present. You had to decide to come tonight before you came. The future, our concept of it, determines our life in the present and life can often be a series of big horizons, each one that justifies the one coming after it. We study at school to get to university or vocational training and that fills our horizon: then the next one, marriage; a home; a better job; ultimately retirement and then? I suppose I've got to die, is that it? According to atheism, that's it. The irony is that atheism claims to give us the big picture from the birth to the death of the cosmos. Yet, in atheism, for the individual human being, death is the ultimate horizon so atheism imprisons human beings, squeezing all of life into an improbably short seventy to eighty years. The acute and powerful comment of the New Testament is that death casts a shadow over all of life. In Hebrews, Christ is described as the One who sets free those who, all their lives, were held in slavery by their fear of death.

One aspect of that freedom that Christ brings is that he puts each of our lives into an immeasurably bigger picture, where the trajectory of our lives does not end at death. Death is a door that leads, for the Christian, to an even bigger experience of the richness of the life that knows no future time boundary. It will ultimately involve the resurrection of the body, at the return of Christ: a return that in itself will lead to the ushering in of a new beginning and the creation of new heavens and a new Earth.

Every chapter of this book ends by bringing the reader up against the next major horizon that this planet will experience; the public return of Jesus Christ our Lord. But this chapter has to do with the relevance of that return to how we cope with physical death. Paul first reminds us that death is a source of real pain and grief. Human death is an intruder; it came into the world through human sin. Indeed, 1 Corinthians 15 says that it is the last enemy that shall be destroyed and that hasn't happened yet. Physical death is still a very real enemy.

We must make very careful distinctions because the Bible uses the word 'death' in several senses. There is physical death but then there is what Scripture calls 'the second death' – that ultimate and final separation from God. That is a death that holds no fear for the believer in Jesus Christ. It has already been conquered in that Christ has given us eternal life and he that believes in him shall never die. Indeed the very Holy Spirit that will one day raise the believer from the dead indwells our bodies but Paul reminds us that they are mortal bodies in which the Holy Spirit dwells. We are still mortal, immortality is not yet.

So physical death remains an enemy and we need to face the fact that death produces grief for all human beings, whether Christian or not. It can shake those who watch it to the core of their beings. Death tears at the human heart. It's important to grieve. Paul says you may not grieve as others do who have no hope but grieve we must. The Lord burst into tears when he saw what death did to Martha,

Mary and Lazarus. Paul writes to channel their grief to be the kind of grief that has hope because he knows that all death raises deep questions of the human heart.

I nearly died last year but the surgeon got to me in time and saved my life. It was very natural for my sister to phone me to say how grateful she was to God. But then last year she lost her twenty-two year old daughter to a brain tumour – just married to a youth pastor. I'm grateful for what God did, and she? Both things have got to be brought under the same God. How is she to understand the devastating loss of a daughter? How's the young husband to cope with the overwhelming grief? How does he square his faith with his emotion?

These are questions that well up in the human heart and can shake the very foundations of our faith. How can God allow it? It's not only death that shakes us, it's often the suffering that proceeds it or the manner of the death. That suffering may be a product of disease or of monstrous human evil. That's why many of my friends do not believe in God. It's the hardest question I face. I don't need only answers for my mind. There are people who are victims of it and they need more than an answer for the mind, they need something that gets down into the heart and the soul.

I'm not going to give you a philosophic discourse about it. I'm going to tell you about something that occurred some time ago in the hope that it might be of some help to you. I visit synagogues often on my travels because I meet people there looking for their identity. I was in the second largest synagogue in the world, in Budapest in Hungary and I met a young South American woman. She was trying to find something to do with her past because her relatives had perished in Auschwitz. The Rabbi was describing an exhibition of the feasts of Israel. She asked me to try to translate for her which was a bit difficult because it was from Yiddish into Spanish. I tried my best but it proved to be a benefit that I wasn't just an expert at Yiddish because I discovered that I was taking a translator's licence and adding to what the Rabbi was saying. I was waxing eloquent and just generally pointing out that Jesus had fulfilled the magnificent festival of Passover and we were getting on fine – until we got to the middle.

I hadn't noticed that in the middle there was a door and above the door, there were three words written in German *Arbeit macht frei* – 'Work will set you free'. It was the door to Auschwitz and behind it there was an exhibition of the most unbelievable cruelty committed on twins in Auschwitz. I'll never forget it, I can see it now and she stood with her hands out like this and in a loud voice she said, 'What does your religion make of this?' There was dead silence. What do you say? I'll tell you what I said. At the end of a long silence, I said, 'I wouldn't insult the memory of your relatives by trying to give you some trivial answer. I have no easy answers. I'm going to ask you to do something very difficult. If we look at this and we say there's no God, then we've solved the problem, haven't we? This is just life and for some it goes well but for very few. For the rest, it's either miserable or wretched and for these children, it was indescribable beyond belief. But that's just the way the world is, so we've satisfied our minds.'

She looked at me very strangely and I said 'So there's no God then. You've solved the problem if you remove God but you haven't removed the suffering. There's one thing you have removed: you've removed all hope. I have a problem because I believe in God and it's going to be difficult. You know I've been talking about the Messiah. I know it's difficult for you but I believe he's God.' She said 'I know that.' I said 'Try to come with me for a moment, to that cross in Jerusalem, all those centuries ago. If that is really God, what is God doing on a cross? There are no trivial answers but that opens up a window for me. I see that God has not remained indifferent to our human suffering but has descended to become part of it.' The tears burst from her eyes as she still stood and she said these unforgettable words, 'Why has no one told me that about my Messiah before?' These are deep questions that we face. There's no other way of beginning to face them than at the cross of Jesus Christ.

Paul wanted to comfort these people because dealing with suffering and death did not end at the cross of Jesus Christ. He wanted to bring them hope. They'd been disturbed and he wanted to talk to them about what death is for the Christian. He calls it 'sleep'. The idea goes back to Jesus himself. He came into the home of Jairus and looked at the little girl on the bed and said, 'She isn't dead, she's only sleeping.' Be careful: we mustn't rush to deduce that since we are unconscious when asleep, the dead are not conscious because the Bible tells us the opposite. 'To be absent from the body' says Paul, 'is to be present with the Lord'. The dead are far from unconscious in that sense but they look asleep.

Paul says that since we believe Jesus has died and rose again, even so, through Jesus, God will bring with him those that have fallen asleep. The Christian view of death is not the product of philosophical meditations on the deep questions of life, it's the product of God's supernatural intervention in raising Jesus from the dead and the logic is powerful. If Jesus is risen from the dead – and he is – then we may be utterly certain that there will be another supernatural intervention and God will bring with Jesus those who have fallen asleep. Paul says (vs15–16): 'we who are alive, who are left until the coming of the Lord will not precede those who have fallen asleep. For the Lord himself will descend from heaven with a cry of command, with the voice of an archangel and with the sound of the trumpet of God.' That colossal sound will break the silence of God for millions of people.

Christ is the first fruits. How did he rise? Not in some metaphorical sense: the ancient Greeks believed in the survival of the soul in some form but when Paul preached to them on the resurrection at Athens, they laughed. They didn't believe in bodily resurrection. But he rose from the dead and he's still human. After the resurrection and ascension, Paul could write these astounding words, 'in him, dwells' – not dwelt – 'all the fullness of the Godhead bodily.' That's such a sharp and clear hope. And the ultimate objective is clear; we shall be caught up together with them in the clouds to meet the Lord in the air and so we will always be with the Lord wherever he is, in this universe or the next. We shall always be with him.

Paul's not finished because there are two kinds of sleep. He's been talking about the sleep of death but now he's going to talk about another kind of sleep: 'concerning the times and the seasons brothers, you've no need for anything to be written to you.'

People get fascinated about the timing of Christ coming. Do they think that if they knew the time, they'd be more willing to get ready for it? The Lord warned of that danger: when the disciples asked him about the time, he said 'Be careful that no-one lead you astray.' Many Christians have spent a lot of time sorting out time tables and trying to fit 1 Thessalonians 4 in with Daniel and the book of Revelation. I don't profess to understand it all but I don't let the difficulty of understanding of all of it stop me believing what Scripture says. If it says that Jesus is going to come and the dead in Christ are going to rise first, I believe that. Never let yourself be robbed by your failure to understand complex things.

Paul is talking about this danger of falling asleep, of not realising that the coming of Christ has to do with moral and spiritual things. Now he changes the phraseology and calls it 'the day of the Lord'. He's talking about judgement and he says that's going to happen unexpectedly and that raises questions in people's minds.

When the disciples asked about the timing, the Lord, in Luke 21, started saying there were going to be a whole sequence of events; wars and rumours of wars; Jerusalem's going to be surrounded by armies and this and that and the other thing. They thought they'd got it all sorted out. Then he changed tack and said 'Watch, be very careful.' Why is that? Because, in an hour you don't think, the Son of Man will come. 'Don't go to sleep' says Christ, 'pray that you may have the strength to escape all these things that are going to take place.'

That's what Paul is saying in 1 Thessalonians 5: 'Don't fall asleep.' And you don't tell people not to fall asleep if they're in no danger of falling asleep. 'Let's be alert and self controlled' he said. 'You're sons of the light; you're sons of the day; you're not sons of the darkness so you should not be behaving as children of the darkness. Let's be alert.'

We need to protect ourselves against going to sleep. The way we can protect ourselves is remembering that we've put on the breast-plate of faith and love and, for a helmet, the hope of salvation. That is those three fundamental Christian virtues: faith, hope and love, the heart of the gospel. If we've got those, they will protect us from falling asleep.

The disciples fell asleep, on several occasions. On that evening when the Lord took his disciples into Gethsemane and said, 'Pray that you don't enter into temptation.' That sleep was such a stupor for Simon. As the minutes ticked past, maybe half an hour later, he found himself in front of a fire and a girl said, 'You were with Jesus, weren't you?' And he said, 'I wasn't.'

Where was the breastplate? Where was the hope? Peter blew his testimony because he had fallen asleep. Was that the end for him? No, the Lord had already prayed for him. Peter's prayer failed but the Lord's prayer didn't.

Are you falling asleep? If you're a genuine believer, the Lord is going to save you, whether you are awake or asleep, so does it matter? In two senses it does. Realism would tell us that if you come into a room and see someone who looks asleep but you find they're like that twenty-four hours later, you would conclude that they're not asleep, they're dead. So when people appear to be asleep, we've got to ask deep questions, don't we? Are they dead or have they just fallen asleep? Are they dead and do they need to be born again? Do they need to repent and trust Christ for salvation and get life in the first place or have they just fallen asleep?

Does it matter? It matters because we're all building. There's only one foundation we can lay and that's already been laid: Christ Jesus. But it's perfectly possible for me to build rubbish: wood, hay and stubble into my life. It'll all have to go. I'll be saved, according to Paul, as though by fire but if I don't build what's valuable into my life and character, it'll all have to go. I've got to appear before the judgement seat of Christ. There's going to be a reward, and it matters how we live; it matters eternally how we live.

Am I asleep? The man who fell asleep, Peter, was the man who shook off his sleep and came into the middle of Jerusalem and launched Christianity on the world. It's why you're here. Who knows what God could do?

A different kind of treasure: Matthew 6:19–24

by Chris Sinkinson

Chris Sinkinson

Chris Sinkinson was converted as a teenager through a college Christian Union. He had wanted to train as an archaeologist and, after work experience with the Test Valley Archaeological Trust, began studying at Southampton University. However, his dislike of standing in cold, wet English fields, coupled with a growing interest in ideas, led him to change direction and study Philosophy and English. After completing a PhD in Theology at Bristol University, he worked with UCCF as a Regional Staff worker for the South West of England. He is now the Pastor of Alderholt Evangelical Church in the New Forest, and lectures part time at Moorlands College in Christchurch. Chris is married and has two boys, Thomas and Toby, who occupy almost all his spare time!

A different kind of treasure: Matthew 6:19–24

As we read from the Bible, it's important to always remember the context. I was told about a wedding where there was a slight hiccup in this. Traditionally it's the best man's duty to read cards from absent friends. On this occasion, there was a reference to the Bible at the foot of the card. The reference was simply 1 John 4:18, which is a lovely verse for a wedding: 'There is no fear in love. But perfect love drives out fear.' However, the best man asked for a Bible to turn the verse up, and turned to John 4:18, and read these words: 'The fact is, you have had five husbands, and the man you now have is not your husband.'

Context is key when we use the Bible. And that's true in the Sermon on the Mount too. The Sermon on the Mount is not some collection of pithy sayings, bundled together. It's a flowing, logical presentation of what it means to be a follower of Jesus in a pagan world. And this passage is about more than money and wealth. It's a key pivot in the Sermon on the Mount. In the first eighteen verses, Jesus has spoken of the danger of religion. Hollow religion can rob us of genuine faith. Religion has a danger. And now from verses 19–34, Jesus will speak of another kind of danger: worldliness. In verses 19–24, the example will be wealth, and then (it's not our passage this evening) verses 25–34 are on worry. Wealth and worry are two ways in which our focus can shift from the God of the Universe to the god of this age.

Jesus has been challenging us not just to talk about faith but to live it out in every area of life in the world where he's placed us. That's been our theme this week and, if we're going to put the Sermon on the Mount into practice, then we will be different. We will be stepping out of our comfort zones, looking different from those in the world around us. As we step out of our comfort zones to apply this, God asks us all a simple question, and I want to show you this question is embedded in the passage.

Do you trust me?

The question God asks us is 'Do you trust me?' Take your attitude to money: just an example. We don't like talking about money, but Jesus spoke a great deal on the subject. Sixteen of the thirty-eight parables deal with money, either by way of an analogy or in a direct way. In Matthew, Mark and Luke, one in every six verses deals with the subject of money, again in one way or another. Why is money so important? Because, if we're honest, we would like a bit more. Why is it that we want more money than we actually need? If we're honest, deep down, it's not about wanting the finest car, the finest house or a lovely swimming pool in the garden . . . Our desire for wealth is about something more profound than that. It is a desire for security. We want to know that we're going to be okay for the future; to be able to provide for our families, our children, our pensions and our grandchildren.

Jesus tells us here that that desire can get in the way of faith. Faith means trust, trusting God. That's why Jesus, a little later on, will turn to the subject of worry. Because if we're going to trust God, we need to let go of security, wealth and worry. It's not that money is the root of all evil. It is the love of money that is a root of all kinds of evil. It leads people into all kinds of sin. Recent research has shown that 80 per cent of households are spending more than their income and, as this credit crunch bites, that's only set to get worse. As somebody put it, 'Too many people are spending money they haven't yet earned, on things they don't need, to impress people they don't like.'

But this passage is about more than money. It is to do with a basic attitude to life. You can be poor and unspiritual, or rich and very spiritual. The question is not how much have you got: it's who do you serve? Where does your trust lie?

A treasure for your heart (vs19–21)

Jesus said 'Do not store up for yourselves treasures on earth, where moth and rust destroy, and where thieves break in and steal.' Material things are doomed. They fade, rot, crumble, corrode, decay, get burned, eaten, stolen, lost, broken. You've got here a very well-rounded description of the things that destroy. There's the animal, moth; the chemical, rust; and the person, thief. If your aim is to stockpile material things, you will never know security or fulfilment. When one of the world's richest men was asked how much money did a man need to be satisfied, the answer was 'Just a little more.' Our society has geared itself to trying to get us to desire more and more. The advertising industry wants you to increase your must-have mentality. As one historian put it 'Advertising has altered humankind. We've gone from caveman and cavewoman to craveman and crave-woman.'

Verse 20: Jesus says 'But store up for yourselves treasures in heaven, where moth and rust do not destroy, and where thieves do not break in and steal.' What is this treasure that really matters? This is something that truly lasts, it's eternal, secure. It's something that nothing can take from us; that means using all that we have in this life to build for the Kingdom of God, one way or another; to know that our income and savings, houses and jobs, even our families, are ours on trust, to use for the glory of God. None of the things around us are going to last: all of it can be used to build for a greater, more eternal purpose. This is the lifestyle that stores up treasures in the very presence of God.

Now I don't understand all of this because Jesus is speaking here of some kind of reward, a treasure that we are storing up before God, that we will know about in the new creation. There's a doctrine of rewards in the Bible, but I can't say I can fully understand it. It's here in Matthew 6:4; 'When you give to the needy, don't let your left hand know what your right hand is doing, so that your giving may be in secret. Then your Father, who sees what is done in secret, will reward you.' It's there in relation to prayer in verse 6, again, 'Then your Father, who sees what is done in secret, will reward you.' Again in verse 18, in relation to fasting, 'Your Father, who is unseen, your Father, who sees what is done in secret, will reward you.' 'He will reward you . . . he will reward you . . . he will reward you.' There is a treasure in heaven. I'm not sure exactly what it is. Maybe it's to do with different responsibilities that we have in the new creation. But we are storing up an eternal reward.

Does that sound a bit mercenary to you? Are we to live a good life because of a reward in eternity? It doesn't sound very Christian . . . Think again.

God is the gift. It is he who will be our treasure. Jesus is our reward. That's why, as Jesus says in verse 21, where your treasure is, there your heart will be also. We have here a motivation to change our lives. What you prize most in life will dictate how you live. Whatever is your greatest treasure, whatever dominates your mind and your thinking, will start dictating to you. Whatever you value most, it captures your heart and ends up governing your life. And if that is Jesus then, as he captures your heart, he governs your life. So if our treasure is eternal, it will capture our hearts. If our treasure is earthly, that too will control us. But our treasure is Jesus. Our reward is the Rewarder, our gift is the Giver.

A light for our eyes (v22)

Verse 22: 'The eye is the lamp of the body: if your eye is good, then your whole body will be full of light.' This is nothing to do with needing the optician; it's nothing to do with good or bad eyes in that sense. We talk about the eye being a window into the soul. Not only is it a window revealing our inner nature, it's also like a lamp. The eye is the lamp of the body, it directs our path, we follow where it leads. If your eyes are always on other things you want, you're going to have little time for God. You'll be following where your eyes lead. If our eyes are fixed on God, then he will direct our lifestyle. Your life will become full of what's good.

The word here that translated 'good' may be translated 'healthy'. Good or healthy, it implies generosity. The same word is used in Romans 12:8 to describe generous giving. It's literally 'good giving'. So it may well be here that good eyes are generous eyes, eyes that see the needs of others more than the needs of the self. And I ask you, what are you training your eyes to see? How are you training your eyes?

The media all around us is trying to train our eyes, to see each other lustfully, to be envious, to laugh at failure, to be cynical of the supernatural, to be blasé about suffering. The world around us is training our eyes to be bad eyes. But to be a different kind of people, we need a different kind of vision, a different set of eyes, a different way of seeing the world.

John Cleese and the Monty Python team wanted to make a comedy about the life of Jesus. So John Cleese and Michael Palin booked a holiday away for a few days and took the gospels to read them through. They read through Matthew, Mark, Luke and John to try and come up with a script. And they found they couldn't do it. They came up with a satire based on a parallel life, called *The Life of Brian*. But why is it they couldn't bring themselves to write the film they intended to make, *The Life of Jesus*? John Cleese said: 'The moment you got really near the figure of Christ, it just wasn't really funny, because Christ was wise, and flexible, and intelligent, and he didn't have any of the things that comedy is about: envy, greed, malice, avarice, lust, stupidity.'

Jesus Christ perfectly reveals to us a life of good eyes. We don't know the colour of his eyes, we don't know the shape of his eyes, but we know they were good eyes. That's visible, demonstrated in his life among us, and that's a contrast with what follows, verse 23: 'But if your eyes are bad, your whole body will be full of darkness. If then the light within you is darkness, how great is that darkness!' The things we watch and look at can determine the kind of people we become.

The word 'good' implies generosity, it shouldn't be surprising that in verse 23 the expression 'the eyes are bad' implies being miserly or envious. I think Jesus is asking us here whether our eyes are full of generosity or envy. When we look at other people or situations, are we full of the desire to bless, give, support and encourage? Or are we full of jealousy, consumed with ourselves? Do we say when we see other people, why have they got all those things? Why do they have those friends? That's bad eyes. That means looking at things and only seeing what we don't have. Remember the little rhyme, 'two men look through the same prison bars, one sees mud, the other sees stars.' We can look at the same situation and see very different things. One sees a reason to be envious and bitter, and another sees the opportunity to bless and give thanks to God.

A master for your life (v24)

In a junior school, a very liberal teacher started to explain her opinions to her class of nine-year-olds, and she told them that she was an atheist. She didn't believe in God. And she asked the class of impressionable nine-year-olds if they were atheists too. Not really knowing what she was talking about, all the hands in the class shot up, except for one. One little girl called Lucy didn't go along with the crowd. 'So what are you?' asked the teacher. 'I'm a Christian,' she answered. The teacher got a bit red-faced and asked her why she was a Christian, and this was her answer. 'I was brought up knowing and loving Jesus. My mum is a Christian, and my dad is a Christian, and I accepted Christ as my Saviour, and so now I am a Christian.' The teacher got a little ruffled. 'That's no reason to be a Christian,' she snapped. 'What if your mum had been stupid and your dad had been stupid, what would you be then?' Without missing a beat, Lucy answered, 'I'd be an atheist.'

I don't actually believe there is such a thing as an atheist. I don't believe it of Richard Dawkins or any other character you care to mention. We all believe in some kind of god. The question is: what god do we believe in? Who is our god? That's what Jesus says here in verse 24, and Paul echoes it in Romans 1–2: there's no such thing as a real atheist. The question is, what do we worship? Who do we worship? Verse 24: 'No one can serve two masters. Either he will hate the one and love the other, or he will be devoted to the one and despise the other. You cannot serve both God and Money.' Hate and love: they're both being used here, not as simple emotional responses. They describe the undivided loyalty that any god would demand. And in that sense, you can only love one.

'Money' is a translation here of the Greek word *mammon*, which implies a kind of god. What is your God? What are you living for? Worldly things? Mammon? Things that are passing away, things that are in a state of decay? Or godly things that are eternal? Paul, in 2 Corinthians 4:18; 'So we fix our eyes not on what is seen, but on what is unseen. For what is seen is temporary, but what is unseen is eternal.' Beauty fades, houses crumble, technology quickly goes out of date and health declines, but Jesus takes his point even further. Mammon doesn't just draw our energies away to invest in futility: mammon strangles our love of God. If we are devoted to one, Jesus says, we will despise the other.

In the rainforests of Borneo, I'm told, there's an unusual and rare kind of tree. It's a species of fig and it's called the Strangler fig tree. Doesn't sound very nice, does it? Birds carry the seeds up into the canopy of the rainforest where the seeds can catch the light. And some of those seeds will take root, up in the canopy of the trees. And the seed then sends its shoots down the trunk of the host until it finally meets the soil and can grow. And as the years go by, more and more roots grow and become thicker. Eventually the host tree is deprived of light, within almost a prison cell of the Strangler tree roots. The tree inside rots away and the fig tree remains. A tiny seed, sown up in the canopy, can deprive the tree it lives on of all its light.

We have got a decision to make. We have to decide where our trust lies. Do we trust God or mammon? If our trust is in wealth, if our security is in something in this world, then as sure as the shoots of the fig tree, it'll spread across our lives. What started out as a little distraction became a mighty dictator, and strangled our love for God. We thought we were surrounded by pleasures and achievements, but we find ourselves in a cage of our own making. We trust in mammon, or we trust in God. God knows what he's doing. All we have, we can recognise as a gift from him. And we can say the Lord gave, the Lord may take away, but blessed be the name of the Lord. We don't have unlimited wealth, but we do have an unlimited God, and I know which one I'd rather trust in.

A different kind of discernment: Matthew 7:1–12

by Steve Brady

Steve Brady

Steve Brady was born in Liverpool, where he was converted in his teens, through a mixture of the Bible and Everton Football Club. He is married with two children and three grandchildren. He has been in full time Christian ministry for over thirty years, is Principal of Moorlands College and a Trustee of Keswick Ministries. He holds a PhD in Theology and is the author of *King of Heaven, Lord of Earth* and *All you need is Christ*, both Keswick study guides, to Colossians and Galatians respectively. A keen sportsman, he hates gardening and still has an irrational attachment to Everton Football Club!

A different kind of discernment:
Matthew 7:1–12

Introduction

There is a view of Christianity that says to be a real Christian is to be utterly and totally naïve. You see the best in everybody. Real Christian faith is non-judgemental, non-discriminatory: any critical faculties you've ever had must be in some way deleterious to Christian faith. In other words, there's a great way to sum up Christians: they are nice people. We just need to be *very* nice people, who actually never see any harm in anybody. And in the real world, where there's lust, violence, war, greed, avarice and injustice, real Christian faith has got not very much to say, because we are called to be 'very nice' people. And when we're in danger of being anything other than that, then the world reminds us of what our Founder said: 'Do not judge, or you too will be judged.' That phrase is not only used out in the world, it's used in the Church as well. There are some terrible abuses going on in local churches: an elder maybe having a relationship with his secretary, sexual abuse going on in some home, or there's a dodgy Sunday school teacher, you're really not sure whether they've been properly police-checked, and then you discover they've got a record of difficulties around children. But you mustn't judge, because Jesus said we mustn't judge. In other words, to be a real Christian is to be basically brain dead, utterly naïve. Isn't that what Jesus said? 'Do not judge, that you be not judged.'

I believe we need a Jesus kind of discernment, because that's what we've got before us in this passage. And I want to bring three main things to you this evening: be careful, be prayerful, and be dareful.

Be careful!

Why do we need this warning from Jesus, 'Do not judge or you too will be judged'? He goes on to talk very strongly about 'you hypocrites.' He's referred to hypocrites before in chapter 6, but now he'll talk about 'you hypocrites.' Why do we need to be careful? Well, at one level, if you read the Sermon on the Mount through, you realise that what Jesus is talking about is utterly and totally impossible. If Mount Sinai, the law, seems difficult, then what Jesus brings before us in the Sermon on the Mount are Himalayan peaks. This is Everest!

Look at the words of Jesus: blessed are those who are pure in heart. Are you totally pure in heart? Who's never felt angry? We'd like to think it was righteous anger, but we know it was just downright pique. And Jesus will go on to talk about lust and many other things. We can go through the Sermon on the Mount and, if we read it properly, come away rightly with a sense of utter failure and despair. To quote St Paul, 'Who is sufficient for these things?' At one level the Sermon works like that. It tells us that there is nobody who could possibly live this kind of Jesus lifestyle. It seems utterly idealistic.

That's what it's supposed to do. At one level, that's why the Sermon on the Mount is a very dangerous document. If we took the Sermon on the Mount out of its gospel context it would be a recipe for despair. At one level, it tells you that you're utterly hopeless and unrighteous. But it goes on to tell you, at another level the great news is God the Rescuer has come to make unrighteous people righteous in his sight, to bring them justification, to give them a righteousness that far exceeds anything that the Pharisees could ever have dreamt of. When that grace of God gets hold of us, when that imputed righteousness that gives us righteousness on credit begins to get hold of us then we do begin, in the words of the Sermon on the Mount and in the Beatitudes, to mourn for our sins and rejoice that Christ has died for us. We do feel poor in spirit, but we know all our riches now are in Jesus. We do live differently, so when we go through all that Jesus says in chapter 5, about murder, adultery, divorce, oaths and an eye for an eye, we say, 'Because of Christ, I don't need to live like that any longer. I've been changed, and I'm being changed. I am now living for a different agenda.'

I've got a purpose far beyond this world. Once I was unrighteous, now in Christ I am righteous! And therein lies the problem, and the danger. Once I've become righteous in Jesus, because our hearts are so complex and so sinful, there is always a danger that self-righteousness will begin to kick in.

I went into a sweetshop here the other day. I got some of these acid drops. They taste horrible. There are always acid drops around the people of God. They're corrosive, censorious and judgemental. They're like that Pharisee in Luke 18. He does everything that he's supposed to do, but his heart is far from God. It's that kind of attitude Jesus was speaking about, that demonises others and in so doing helps to deify yourself. The Church has never been short of self-righteousness.

So is Jesus saying that we shouldn't judge, and therefore we should just be nice? Notice the context, the wonderful balance of Scripture. Jesus says: 'It will be measured to you this way. If you want a smile, you give somebody a smile. If you grimace at people, they'll probably grimace back. But look,' he says, 'why do you look at the speck of sawdust in your brother's eye and pay no attention to the plank in your own?' Is he saying you're not to do anything about it? No. 'You hypocrite, first take the plank out of your own eye.' How do you do that if you don't make some judgement?

Jesus is not calling us to a naïve gullibility; he's calling us to see *through* things and people, to weigh motives. So when you come across somebody who's got a problem, you don't write them off. They may have a speck in their eye, but of course it's no good trying to help them if you've got a plank in your own. At that point, you do not need Specsavers, you need Casualty.

Note he doesn't say 'Mind your own business' or 'You're all sinners and nobody can do anything about it in the church.' All that kind of nonsense that goes on in local church life: somebody's in gross sin, but nobody does anything because 'We're all sinners.' What the Lord Jesus is reminding us of is that when we do come across problems with other people, we had better make sure that we ourselves have sorted out difficulties in our own hearts. Galatians 6:1 springs to mind: 'Brothers, if someone is caught in a sin, you who are spiritual should restore him gently. But watch yourself, or you also may be tempted.' It means mend them, in a spirit of gentleness, but consider yourself lest you also be tempted. It's the picture of gentleness, of the wounded healer, coming to somebody who does have a problem with their eye. But before you can sort it out, like a wise surgeon, you've got to make sure you've scrubbed up and sterilised, because otherwise you can do damage. It's a very delicate operation, getting anywhere near the eye. Most of us don't like people messing around with our eyes.

This is not a call to ignore something wrong, it's calling for discernment, so when something is wrong, we come with the meekness and gentleness of Christ. And if I'm going to help somebody else I'd better make sure that that grace of God is so at work in my own heart that I come with a sweetness and gentleness to deal with that person with the problem.

Then Jesus adds something which is again intriguing. 'Do not give dogs what is sacred; do not throw your pearls to pigs. If you do, they may trample them under their feet, and then turn and tear you to pieces' (Mt. 7:6). The pigs or the dogs? It's hard to know. It's a warning that some folk do seem almost beyond help. This is a metaphor of people: the Early Church often used this to guard the Lord's table, to keep unbelievers away. The Lord Jesus is reminding us that some people are incredibly hard to reach, and do present an incredibly hard shell. Some come over as incredibly against the gospel and are violent. Jesus says: 'Therefore, you're not to give them what's sacred; there are times when you've got to shake off the dust from your feet.'

I've always found it a very difficult thing to know when to do that. Because some people are incredibly difficult. Of course, first perceptions are not always the truth, are they? I remember knocking on a guy's door in east London. He said, 'What d'you want?' I said, 'I've come to tell you about Jesus.' He said, 'I'm not interested.' I said, 'What is it you're not interested in, because I think knowing Jesus is the most wonderful thing in the world.' He said, 'I don't believe in him.' I said, 'What are you then, an atheist?' He said, 'Yeah, I'm an atheist.' I said, 'Let me congratulate you then, you've got to have a lot of faith to be an atheist.' He said, 'Oh nah. It's not like that at all mate. Science has disproved God.' I said, 'What branch of science has disproved God?' He said, 'Evolution.' I said, 'Are you into macro or micro evolution?' He said, 'What? Look, I'm having me dinner, come back tomorrow.' So I came back the next night and spent four hours with Lee, an 'ard man from the East End of London, who had a black belt in karate, talking about the God he didn't believe in. We agreed on one thing: I didn't believe in his God either, because he didn't exist. Over a period of months this hard nut came to faith in Christ.

In March I met a lovely young lady. I'd been introduced to her by her boyfriend, a believer, and she wasn't. He wanted me to meet her because she'd just been diagnosed with lung cancer. She said, 'I don't get it about all this Jesus stuff at all.' A couple of weeks later, she came round with her boyfriend to have a look at the college. And as we're going round our library, she says, 'You haven't got a book in this library about how to become a Christian, have you?'

Over the next half hour as we shared the gospel, Annie came to Christ in a lovely way. It wasn't long afterwards Rex, her fiancé now, said, 'I think we need to be married, she's not very well.' We had a wonderful day, with loads of non-Christians there, and at the end of that day we thought she might have two years. She was fighting for breath. We married her on a Saturday, and on the following Tuesday she lost the battle and died. I buried her the next week in sure and certain hope of a resurrection to eternal life. You never know when a door of opportunity's going to open. We need to be discriminating. We need to be careful.

We need to be prayerful

Why does this follow on here? How come we're back to prayer: asking and seeking and knocking? I suspect that one reason is because it's only as we keep close to God that we're going to be able to not only see things but see through things, to be wise and discerning, to be able to evaluate and critique, and discriminate without becoming judgemental. And there's all sorts of problems around prayer. After all, doesn't Matthew 6:32 tell us God knows already, so if God knows already, then what are we telling him for? We need to recapture verse 11: 'your Father in heaven'. Prayer is about relationships: not about getting my will done. Prayer is about God getting his will done through me. Often when I go to God, the real issue is: Lord, what is it you want to do in me and through me, rather than my just saying well I want you to do this, that and the other.

Yet it seems here that Jesus is saying: 'But you can ask, seek, and knock.' If there's an order here, I suspect it's one of growing in intensity, of asking. These are all what we call present imperatives in the Greek: it means keep on asking. Keep seeking, putting your heart and soul into it, hungering and thirsting after righteousness, and keep knocking. There's some things you keep asking God about.

Have you ever been in a testimony meeting where somebody gets up and says, 'I want to give a real testimony. I was really praying for this thing, really pleading with God, and I was asking and seeking and knocking and guess what? The Lord said "No!"'? It's an answer to prayer, isn't it? Have you ever said 'No' to your kids? If you haven't, you're a poor parent. And there are many other times when God simply says, 'Wait.' I think of the dear man who, for nearly forty years, prayed for his wife. After nearly forty years of prayer, she came to faith in Christ, and I had the joy of seeing her profess this in the waters of baptism.

What is it that God is giving? The ultimate reward that God gives is himself. One day God's going to gather his children in his arms and say, 'You are mine.'

Be dareful (v12)

So how does verse 12 fit in then, as we close? Some commentators say verse 12 doesn't follow on, yet the original says 'therefore'. What's the 'therefore' there for? When you know that once upon a time you were an unrighteous person, outside the grace of God, and you've tasted the goodness and mercy of the Lord, and grace starts working in your life, you start to become a different person. You start to live the Jesus way out of gratitude. Some of the old theologians used to call the doctrine of sanctification, being made holy, the doctrine of gratitude. It's your life saying: 'Lord, here I am! I'm wholly available to you. Lord, I'm sorted out with you, you're my heavenly Father, nothing is ever going to be able to separate me from your love in Christ so Hallelujah, Lord, here I am! Wholly available!' And that's why we can therefore be dareful.

These words of Jesus are echoed in other ethical systems. Confucius says, 'What you do not want done to yourself, do not do to others.' The Stoics said, 'What you do not wish to be done to you, do not do to anyone else.' They're fairly negative. That won't do for Jesus. Jesus puts it positively. He doesn't say, 'Don't do any harm.' He says, 'So in everything do to others what you'd have them do to you. Take the initiative, for this sums up the law and the prophets.' What sums up the law and the prophets? It's the law of love, isn't it? If God has done all this for me in Jesus Christ, then I can go and make a difference for him. I'm not going to be like the rich man who lets the poor man sit at my gate, I'm not going to be like the priest and the Levite who walk by on the other side of the road and leave it to a Samaritan, I'm not going to be like that servant in Matthew 25 who buries his talent in the ground. Real Christian faith is a living faith, it's an active faith, it makes me different. It gives me a holy dare. So like the eighteenth century John Wesley, do all the good you can, by all the means you can, in all the places you can, at all the times you can, to all of the people you can, as long as you ever can!

Our evangelical forebears were busy people for the Kingdom. He'd seen hundreds of thousands of people converted but not long before his death, William Booth, said these words: 'While women weep as they do, I'll fight. While men go into prison, in and out, in and out, I'll fight. While little children go hungry as they do, I'll fight. While there remains one dark soul without the light of the gospel, I will fight and I'll fight to the end!' That's what it's about. We are men and women impacted by the power of God, men and women of purpose and destiny who are determined to go out, get out of our comfort zones, go and do something vital for Jesus. God, I believe, is calling many of us to get out of our comfort zones. Let's go and do something outrageously good, totally unexpected, where discernment, of course, born out of love for Jesus, is the order of the day. And then people will begin to sit up and take notice. Because the world is watching, and the world is waiting. The world is needing individual Christians and communities of believers who do outrageously good things because they're responding to the outrageous grace of God, that has touched them, and reached them and brought them into the Jesus family, forevermore.

Behold the Throne: Revelation 4
by *Paul Mallard*

Paul Mallard

Paul Mallard has served as Senior Pastor at Woodgreen since 1995. He is zealous for teaching the Bible so it is really understood and applicable to life today. He believes training a new generation of Christian leaders is very important. Paul served as the President of the Fellowship of Independent Evangelical Churches (FIEC) from April 2004 to August 2007. Paul is married to Edrie and they have four children: two boys, Caleb and Amos, and two girls, Keziah and Emmaus. He still feels a great affection for Birmingham where he was born and brought up, and is a keen West Bromwich Albion supporter.

Behold the throne: Revelation 4

Introduction

The gift of encouragement is one of the greatest things in our churches today. Pastors, ministers, vicars; they all need encouragement. Your church leaders need encouragement. There's probably not a single Christian who doesn't need encouragement. The apostle John was a man who, when he received the words of Revelation, needed encouragement. Things were not going well in his life or in the life of the Church. If ever they needed a word of encouragement, it was now. And into this situation came the book of Revelation.

The Book of Revelation is designed to bring encouragement to the hearts of God's people. We often get the Book of Revelation wrong. We think it's a desperately difficult book to understand, but it's not a kind of spiritual Sudoku. It's not a code book. The Book of Revelation is a picture book, and the aim is to remove the veil and show us God, in all his glory. In the end, the Lamb is going to win. That was the encouragement that John needed, that we need, and the encouragement that comes from Revelation 4. What I want to do is to draw your attention to three aspects of this heavenly throne. It is a place of authority (vs 1–2); a place of awe (vs 3–7); and a place of adoration (vs 8–11).

A place of authority (vs 1–2)

'After this I looked, and there before me was a door standing open in heaven.' Chapter 4 comes naturally after chapters 2 and 3, which is where the Lord gives the Church a spiritual check-up. There are lots of wonderful things to commend, but there are also some serious problems and challenges. The Church is under attack: virtually all of the seven churches are facing persecution. They're being invaded by false teachers, men who bring what he calls 'the deep teaching of Satan.' As Christians, we should always be suspicious of people, I suggest, who bring things that we've never seen in the Bible before. If no one has ever seen it before, it's probably because it wasn't there. But the most alarming thing of all is the spiritual decline within the churches that is almost bordering on apostasy.

What does he say to the church at Ephesus? 'You were going so well, there are so many things to commend you, but there's one thing, and it is so dreadful, I'm on the point of removing you, the Church. You don't love me like you used to.' When I was converted, when I first became a Christian, I was desperately in love with Jesus. Can you remember when you loved him more?

The Lord looks at the church in Ephesus and says 'It's so sad that you've lost your first love, that you don't love me like you used to.' And to the church in Sardis, 'You have such a fantastic reputation! Everybody's talking about how alive you are, but it's only a reputation. You're spiritually dead.' Worst of all, to the church at Laodicea: 'You're so compromised, you make me sick.' Poor old John, you can imagine him thinking, as he looks at the Church and listens to the word of the Lord, 'Has the Church got a future?' It's after these things that God takes him to heaven and shows him this great and glorious vision.

What's the point of this vision? It's simply that even when the Church is feeble, even when the world seems to turn its back on God completely, the ultimate place of authority in the universe is the Throne of God. And it is occupied. It's never been unoccupied. Indeed, the word 'throne' is one of the key words in Revelation. It is used about sixty times in the New Testament, 47 times in the Book of Revelation and fourteen times in this chapter. The theme of the chapter, of Revelation and indeed the whole Bible, is the absolute authority of the throne of God. The Church is in a state, things are going badly, but God is still on the throne.

So often when we think about God, we have this picture in our mind of this small God, who looks upon the universe, wondering what he can do. God doesn't look at the universe and get frustrated, he doesn't wring his hands. There's a throne! And the throne is occupied. God has plans for his cosmos, his Church, and for you. Maybe you have trials and troubles. You need to take this to heart: God is still on the throne. Your children are in God's hands. Your church is in God's hands. There is a God in heaven, and he reigns and he loves you.

When we go through trials, what's our first conclusion? God's abandoned me, God doesn't love me any more, God's turned his back. Don't you realise that even in the most dreadful trial, God still loves you? Indeed, those whom the Lord loves, he chastens. The sign of love is that the Lord loves us and chastens us. And it is the sovereign God who has the authority over the whole universe; who has John in his hand, and the Church in his hand, and you in his hand tonight. The sovereignty of God is the softest pillow on which Christians can bow their heads.

A place of awe (vs 3–7)

John gives us a tour of the throne room of heaven. Notice the throne is at the centre of everything. The overwhelming impression is one of majesty, awe and wonder. We may not all agree on the details, but Revelation is saying 'Look at the awesome, awful, awe-inspiring majesty of God.' Who is the one on the throne? 'And the one who sat there had the appearance of jasper and carnelian. A rainbow, resembling an emerald, encircled the throne.' In Revelation 1, when John is describing Christ in his majesty and glory, he says he's like 'a son of man.' Jesus still has his humanity. When he went back to heaven, he didn't leave his humanity behind. But when John describes the Father, the one who sits on the throne, he can't use those kinds of pictures. The finite human language struggles to get around it. He has the appearance, says John, of something like an emerald rainbow. It's a picture of beauty, majesty, the one who dwells in light.

A couple of years ago, my wife and I celebrated our 25th wedding anniversary, and we ended up in the Swiss Alps, just across the way from Mont Blanc. I was looking out at the mountains. Suddenly the clouds parted and the sun came out, and the light of the sun hit the snow on top of Mont Blanc. I glanced up, and just for a moment I was blinded. I couldn't bear to look at the bright lights. Now, if a little bit of light coming from the sun, hitting a few crystals of ice, produces near blindness for a second, what do you think the majesty and the glory of God is like?

Surrounding the throne were 24 other thrones, and seated upon them were 24 elders. What do these elders represent? They represent the totality of the redeemed community. In Revelation 21, John sees the New Jerusalem – it has twelve gates that represent the twelve tribes. It has twelve foundations, that represent the twelve apostles. It's the people of God from the Old Testament, and the people of God from the New Testament, and they're joined together around the throne. As you go on (v4) it tells us they were dressed in white and they had crowns of gold on their heads. They are the redeemed of Christ, redeemed by his blood, dressed in white robes. They're the ones who reign with Christ: his victor's crown upon their heads. The closest to the throne in heaven are those who represent the redeemed community. Isn't that encouraging? The Church, the people of God, are closest to his heart. Sometimes we get disillusioned with the Church. It is very easy to be critical of the Church. Be careful when you criticise the Church, because it's his Church.

John describes (v5) 'flashes of lightning, rumblings and peals of thunder' coming from the throne. In Greek, it's in the present tense, they're *constantly* coming. It's a picture of the holiness of God. Just as at Sinai the ground shook, and the air was filled with light, it is a picture of the holiness of God. It's a fearful thing to fall into the hands of the living God. And it goes on 'Before the throne, seven lamps were blazing. These are the seven spirits of God.' That's the way in which God in his symbolic will speaks of the Holy Spirit. There aren't seven spirits. The seven is a picture of the fullness of the Holy Spirit. As we read through chapters 4 and 5, we see the grand mystery of the Trinity: the Father on the throne, before the throne the Spirit of God, and the Lamb who was slain in chapter 5. Also before the throne (v6) there is a 'sea of glass,' which speaks of blazing purity. Then in verse 6, in the midst of the throne – whatever that means – there are 'four living creatures, and they were covered with eyes, in front and in back' – this speaks of of knowledge and understanding.

> The first living creature was like a lion, the second was like an ox, the third had a face like a man, the fourth was like a flying eagle. Each of the four living creatures had six wings and was covered with eyes all around, even under his wings. Day and night they never stop saying: "Holy, holy, holy is the Lord God Almighty, who was, and is, and is to come" (Rev. 4:7–8).

Maybe the most striking picture of all is in this vision of these creatures. They've got four faces like the cherubim in Ezekiel 1, six wings like the seraphim in Isaiah 6. What is it that they represent? I believe they represent the animate creation that God has made. The lion represents the wild beasts, the ox represents the domestic beasts, the eagle represents the flying beasts and man, as the height, the climax of creation, represents the last piece that God puts into the jigsaw. This is the picture of the whole of creation, praising God. The whole of creation joins the redeemed in heaven, to worship God. What's the overall impression we have? The flashes of lightning, the sounds of thunder, the movement of angels . . . It's a picture of awe and mystery, majesty and wonder. Are you looking forward to heaven? It's going to be glorious.

When my oldest daughter was a little girl, she fell in love with elephants – I think we'd shown her the film *Dumbo*. So everything was elephants. We had books about elephants, we had stuffed toys, we had pictures on the walls, and so we decided one day that we'd take her along to Bristol Zoo to show her the real thing. We pushed her into the enclosure where the elephants were, twisted the buggy around and, for the very first time, she saw elephants in the flesh. She'd seen the books, she's seen the pictures, but this was the very first time when she was face-to-face with this huge creature that filled her whole vision. I'll never forget her response. She looked up at this creature, and her jaw dropped open, and she said 'Oh, wow!' When you see the reality, it's overwhelming. The reality of God, the reality of the throne room of heaven is so awesome and so breathtaking because God is glorious. God is beautiful and breathtaking, mighty and majestic, magnificent and mysterious, and we need in these days desperately to recapture the fear of the Lord. We can't be familiar with God, he's not a mate. God is glorious. The fear of the Lord is the beginning of wisdom. The throne is a place of authority, and a place of awe.

A place of adoration (vs 8–11)

Every picture of heaven that is revealed in Revelation always speaks about the worship of heaven, the adoration of the one who's on the throne and the Lamb. It is constant adoration (v8): 'Each of the four living creatures had six wings and was covered with eyes all around, even under his wings. Day and night they never stop saying: "Holy, holy, holy is the Lord God Almighty, who was, and is, and is to come."' Constantly, around the clock, they exist to worship God. It's a constant, God-centred adoration (v9–10): 'Whenever the living creatures give glory, honour and thanks to him who sits on the throne and who lives for ever and ever, the twenty-four elders fall down before him who sits on the throne, and worship him who lives for ever and ever.' They lay their crowns before the throne. It's all about God. As we heard earlier, it's not about how I feel, or what I enjoy, it's about God. It's all about the throne, it's about the majesty and wonder of God. And the creation, represented by the four living creatures, and the redeemed, represented by the 24 elders, lift up their hearts in praise and worship. It is wonderfully, gloriously joyful.

There's a lovely story about when Spurgeon was pastoring at the Metropolitan Tabernacle in London. In those days, he would always get very enthusiastic, there was a great joy in his preaching, and somebody came from a stricter church, and they came into the Metropolitan Tabernacle. They didn't like what happened there, so they left and they wrote a letter to Mr Spurgeon, saying, 'We came to your church on Sunday, and we didn't like the way it was. We're going to go and find a church which is more suitably miserable.' But it's not like that. It's adoration, it's praise! We need to recapture that wonder of God, how to respond with praise. We were created for adoration. We were redeemed for adoration. We are destined for adoration. And it's all about him, not how we feel. Sometimes in our Christian lives we lose our adoration, we lose our worship, we lose that sense of the wonder of God.

I've got a friend who's very busy in ministry. His wife says when he dies, she's not going to put 'R.I.P' on his grave, she's going to put 'G.T.A.M': 'Gone To A Meeting.' You can be diligent in your religion, and distant in your relationship. When was the last time when the wonder and the glory and the majesty of God captured your heart, and you were thrilled?

Who is he (v8)?

As we close, let me focus on just two aspects of what this chapter tells us about God: who he is (v8) and what he's done (v11). The most simple, profound, fundamental truth about God is his holiness. It's the sheer *Godness* of God, it's what marks him out as God: his awesome majesty, his absolute purity, holy is the Lord. He's the God who is Almighty. The Greek word there is *pantokrator*, *pan* which means everything, *krator* means grasp. He is the God who grasps and grips everything. He grasps the cosmos, he grasps the stars and the mountains and the oceans and the planets, he grasps the Church, he grasps you. The Holy One, the Almighty One, the Eternal and Unchanging One, who was and who is and who is to come. We are creatures of a moment. John is an old man in his nineties, and he stands before the eternal God. We're dust and ashes, and he is the eternal one. We need to get a greater vision of who God is.

What has he done (v11)?

We need to get a greater vision of what God has done. Here's the climax of the whole chapter (v11)

> "You are worthy, our Lord and God,
> to receive glory and honour and power,
> for you created all things,
> and by your will they were created
> and have their being."

God created everything out of nothing, by the power of his word and for the purpose of his glory. The whole of the cosmos begins with God, belongs to God, and exists because God wills it, and will one day glorify God. And the purpose of Revelation 4 is to lift our eyes to the throne, and to lift our eyes to what God has made and say, 'Wow! What a God.'

Look up at the stars. Here we are in the Milky Way, which is a city of stars. We're a little rock, third rock from the Sun. The Sun belongs to the Milky Way. How many stars in the Milky Way? In the Milky Way there are a hundred billion stars, in just our cluster. If you want to count them, one a second, 24 hours a day, seven days a week, it would take you three thousand years to count the stars in the Milky Way. But the Milky Way is one of one hundred billion galaxies. A hundred billion clusters of stars out there in the cosmos. It's the greatest understatement in Scripture, Genesis 1:16, 'he made the stars also.' Without breaking a sweat, he cast billions of stars into space.

I was preaching at Oxford University a couple of years ago, and they gave me Psalm 19, and I wanted to impress them there, so I looked up a statistic, and it was that if you look at the number of people on the Earth, there are something like six and a half billion people on Earth. If you wanted to divide the stars amongst the people, every single man and woman on the Earth would get, according to my statistics, one *trillion* stars. So I gave this statistic and I was very proud of myself, until afterwards a man came to me and said, 'I teach in the astrophysics department, and your statistic was dramatically wrong. If you were to divide the stars in the universe amongst the people on the planet, each person on the planet would not get one trillion stars. Each person on the planet would get 2.3 trillion stars.' Be that as it may, here is John, and he's in trouble, the Church is in trouble, and God says to him, 'Look at the throne. Look at the power of God. Look at the majesty of God. Look at the might of God.' It's a place of authority, it's a place of awe, it's a place of adoration. 'John, lift up your eyes, lift up your heart. All is well.'

Behold the Church: Revelation 7

by John Risbridger

John Risbridger

John Risbridger has been at Above Bar Church in Southampton since September 2004, serving as Minister and Team Leader. He loves Bible teaching and student work, and is passionate about the interface of worship, theology and music. Growing up in a Christian home, John grew into an active faith at a young age. After five years in hospital management, he joined UCCF in 1994, working first as a regional team leader and then as Head of Student Ministries. John is a Trustee of Keswick Ministries. He is married to Alison and they have two daughters. His favourite leisure pursuits include spending time with his family, walking, eating curry and listening to music of all kinds.

Behold the Church: Revelation 7

Introduction

Behold the Church, what do you see? Look across the world and, in nation after nation, you'll see the Church as a small oppressed minority: persecuted and impoverished. The other day I had a copy of the Barnabas Fund magazine come through my letterbox. I read it for about ten minutes while I was having my lunch. Ten minutes of reading that will tell you of Christians arrested and churches closed in Algeria, after a few years of relative freedom. It will tell you about forced conversions to Islam in Uzbekistan and Iraq. It will tell you about Christians starving in Burma after the cyclone. Behold the Church, what do you see? You see it opposed and suffering. But does that surprise you? It shouldn't; not if we've read the book of Revelation. The churches to whom this prophecy was first addressed faced exactly the same problems. In chapters 1 to 3, they're addressed, one after the other. It is the reality of a beleaguered and struggling Church that provides the background to our chapter.

The Four Horsemen

It's all set out in chapter 6, which we don't have time to look at in detail, but let me highlight the opening verses there where the Lamb breaks open the seals. As the first four seals are opened, four horsemen

ride out onto the face of the Earth. The first horseman is riding a
white horse, it appears good and wholesome but its agenda is conquest
and destruction. Probably this is a picture of false teaching. The second
rider rides out on a fiery red horse and it stirs up conflict and hatred.
The third comes out on a black horse which brings famine and hard-
ship, and the fourth comes on a pale horse and its rider is death. In a
sense the fourth horse is the conclusion of the other three. The
destructive impact of these four horsemen and what they represent is
felt by many across the globe but it seems that the Church bears the
brunt. That's what the fifth seal suggests with its pictures of the mar-
tyrs under the altar (vs 9-11), crying out, 'How long must the Church
suffer?' So you read through chapter 6 and find yourself asking the
question 'Will the Church of Jesus Christ survive all these assaults?'

Whenever you do ask that question – it is to Revelation 7 that we
must turn. The chapter invites us to behold the Church from a wholly
different perspective, the perspective of God himself and we get that
perspective through the two distinct visions which make up chapter 7.

The seal of God (vs 1–8)

The vision has changed from a vision of four horsemen to a vision
of four angels holding back the four winds on the world. But the
reality that this vision is describing is the same because the winds
are destructive in their impact, like the four horsemen were.
They're bringing harm to creation and potentially to the Church.
Verse 1

> After this I saw four angels standing at the four corners of the
> earth, holding back the four winds of the earth to prevent any
> wind from blowing on the land or on the sea or on any tree. Then
> I saw another angel coming up from the east, having the seal of the
> living God. He called out in a loud voice to the four angels who
> had been given power to harm the land and the sea: "Do not harm
> the land or the sea or the trees until we put a seal on the foreheads
> of the servants of our God."

So we've got the four angels, the four winds, bringing destruction and then this fifth angel appears instructing the other four to hold fire until God's servants have received his seal.

Here are these a hundred and forty-four thousand and who are they? I'm going to tell you what I think. You can disagree with me, as long as you do it nicely. They are God's servants (v3): 'Do not harm the land or the sea or the trees until we put a seal on the foreheads of the servants of our God.'

This is the same body of people that Revelation was originally addressed to. It's described as having been written for his servants, to show what must soon take place (Rev. 1:1). And if you look through Revelation, at every occasion where people are called 'God's servants', you will find that this is not some special in-crowd, this is the whole of God's servants. You will also find that, time and again, Old Testament language which is associated with Israel is being applied to the whole believing community – both Jew and Gentile. So again, right at the beginning, 'To him who loves us and has freed us from our sins by his blood, and has made us to be a kingdom and priests to serve his God and Father' (Rev. 1:5–6). The picture and the language is drawn straight out of Exodus 19, speaking about Israel, but in Revelation, it's applied to the Church of Jesus Christ.

That's exactly what is going on here, with the hundred and forty-four thousand sealed from Israel. How do you make a hundred and forty four? Well, it's twelve times twelve; twelve tribes, twelve apostles. So the hundred and forty-four thousand is the believing community of the people of God in its completeness, Jew and Gentile alike. And they are all given the seal of the living God by this fifth angel.

What then is the seal? The seal is a seal of ownership and protection. A year or two ago I went to Word Alive, and when we arrived, we were all given orange wrist bands. Have you been to conferences where you've had to wear one of these wrist bands? And once you've got it on, you're not allowed to take it off for the whole of the conference. The wrist band is, if you like, a seal. It's saying 'You belong here and therefore you're protected.' That's exactly the point of the seal here in Revelation. God is saying, 'They're mine and I'm taking care of them.'

Paul spoke of something very similar in 2 Corinthians 1:21–22:'it is God who makes both us and you stand firm in Christ. He anointed us, set his seal of ownership on us, and put his Spirit in our hearts as a deposit, guaranteeing what is to come.' Do you see how closely that ties up with what John is talking about here? It's something given to all God's people and this is a seal of protection, given so that we stand firm in Christ. It's a seal of ownership, but the seal isn't an 'it' at all – the seal is a Person, the personal presence of God living in his people by his Holy Spirit. Does the Church have a future? Will the Church survive the four horsemen; the four winds; the taunts of Richard Dawkins; the agenda of political correctness? Does the Church have a future? The answer is yes because God has sealed his people with his own presence with his Holy Spirit – the seal of ownership, of protection.

Richard Bauckham, who's one of the most important influential scholars on Revelation, has pointed out that in the Old Testament, censuses were always used to determine the military strength of the nation. And the phrase that's used in the listing of the census here (where it says 'from the tribe of') is almost identical to the phrase used in the military census in Numbers 1. Why is that important? This picture of the hundred and forty-four thousand sealed is not some passive bunch of people sitting back thinking, 'I'm sealed so I'm okay.' This is a picture of an army, a fighting force of holy warriors resolutely defying the opposition, as they stand firm in the name of Christ; an army which has the protection of God over it.

Men

I've taken a lot of risks tonight so I might as well take another one. Can I address the men among us for a moment? How many of us are weary of the fluffy bunnies version of the Christian faith? Everyone being nauseatingly nice; singing love songs to Jesus; no conviction; no drive; no compelling motivating vision of living for something else, of something to aim for, something to achieve? I believe there's something profound that we men need to recover: this biblical metaphor of a calling to be holy warriors, an army standing firm for Jesus. The fluffy bunnies version of Christianity is not the only version that's around. There's also a calling to sign up and make a difference in the world, for Jesus' sake. The women need to hear that too but from what I see, generally the women are doing it already. We're in the process of sending out some new mission partners in our church at present and they're women. It's wonderful that they are women but where are the guys who are saying 'I want to make a difference for Jesus in the world'?

The second vision

Why would you do it? What is this goal that's worth living for? Chapter 6 finishes like this 'They called to the mountains and the rocks, "Fall on us and hide us from the face of him who sits on the throne and from the wrath of the Lamb! For the great day of their wrath has come, and who can stand?"'

Let that question echo round this tent: who can stand? Who can stand against all the opposition? Who can even stand when the very judgement of God falls? The answer is there in chapter 7:9, where John says; 'After this I looked and there before me was a great multitude that no one could count, from every nation, tribe, people and language, standing before the throne and in front of the Lamb.' What are they doing? They are standing before the throne, in front of the Lamb. It's the same throne and the same Lamb that has moved over the Earth in judgement. This is a picture of the salvation of God, of the Church now rewarded in glory, going all the way through from verses 9 to 17.

What is your vision?

God's plan is to save a huge multitude of people and you get something of the sense of the sheer scope of the plan here. God's plans for salvation are expansive and international. What is your vision of the Church? Is it of a comfortable little bunch of people rather like you, who are going to help you defend things the way they've always been, as together you make your own untroubled way to heaven?

Revelation 7 screams against that kind of narrow thinking and cries to us to give up our small ambitions for the Christian Church. Our business is the glory of the Lamb, and Revelation tells us that the glory of the Lamb demands the saving of a vast multitude from every nation. This is God's vision for the Church. Is it your vision?

What are they celebrating (vs 10–12)?

They're holding palm branches, a symbol of victory and now they're standing in front of the throne of God and they're celebrating. But their song is not one of self congratulation. Instead they cry (v10) 'Salvation belongs to our God, who sits on the throne, and to the Lamb.' That's what makes them rejoice. And as they cry out their praise to God, it's as if the whole of heaven erupts (v11): 'All the angels were standing around the throne and around the elders and the four living creatures. They fell down on their faces before the throne and worshiped God.' What is the heartbeat of heaven's worship? What should be the heartbeat of our worship? The thing that ignites the praise of heaven is the fulfilment of God's great salvation plan and the achievement of the Lamb who was slain.

What is their story (vs 13–14)?

'These are they who have come out of the great tribulation'. Their trust was that Jesus was the Lamb of God, who loved them and freed them from their sins by his blood and so, (v14), 'they have washed their robes and made them white in the blood of the Lamb.' It's a strange image. Normally if you spill blood on clothes, it stains them. The blood of Jesus doesn't stain, it removes stains, it cleanses, it makes us perfectly white because his blood is the blood of sacrifice. Those who are cleansed by his blood are clothed in the radiance of his righteousness; standing here before the throne of God, with their robes made white, a symbol of purity, of having triumphed through faith in Christ. So now they stand before the throne of God, holy in his sight, without blemish and free from accusation.

What is their future (vs 15–17)?

As John sees them now, they are before the throne of God and serve him day and night. They are experiencing the presence of God, joining in the worship of heaven. But when you get into verses 16 and 17, the tense changes – it's now a future tense. We are getting a glimpse of the very end of the book of Revelation, the climax of history, when heaven comes to Earth and God makes all things new. I'm convinced that too often we have spoken of heaven as some far away place where we live a ghostly kind of existence as shadows of our former selves. I want to suggest to you that biblical hope puts it exactly the opposite way round: what we are now is a mere shadow of our future selves. Real humanity is what we're going to experience then, in the new heaven and the new Earth, when we're living life in a new creation with God.

And so John describes it (v16), 'Never again will they hunger; never again will they thirst. The sun will not beat upon them, nor any scorching heat.' Why no more need? Because (v17), 'For the Lamb at the centre of the throne will be their shepherd'. They're safe because they have the perfect shepherd – who has been a lamb himself. The shepherd, who has great power because he is at the centre of the throne, gave his life for them as the Lamb of God, who takes away the sins of the world. With the Lamb as their shepherd, they look forward to glorious unending life. He will lead them to springs of living water, the water of life which flows from the throne of God.

'And God will wipe away every tear from their eyes.' It's one of the most glorious images of Scripture. It doesn't say that God will give them a tissue. This is a far more intimate picture. God will wipe away every tear from their eyes – an extraordinary picture of intimate care and eternal healing, as the grief, the losses, the set backs, the disappointments of a lifetime are wiped away in the healing compassion of God, the great Shepherd. This is the future of the Church of Jesus Christ and if you're part of the Church, this is your future and it's the only future that's worth living for, that in the end will not be whittled away in futility. Here is something worth living for and God's great passion is that this future should be shared not by a select few from here and there but by a vast multitude from every nation of the Earth. That is the plan and purpose of God and is that your plan too?

Keswick 2008

CDs, DVDs, tapes, videos and books

All talks recorded at Keswick 2008, plus many more audio and
video recordings from the Convention, dating back to 1957,
can be ordered from

www.essentialchristian.com

or by calling ICC: 01323 643341
Fax 01323 649240

Resource catalogues featuring recent audio and video recordings of
the Keswick Convention, including much that is not covered in
this book, can be obtained from

can be obtained from ICC

Some previous annual Keswick volumes (all published by
STL/Authentic Media) can be obtained from:
The Keswick Convention Centre
Skiddaw Street, Keswick, Cumbria, CA12 4BY
Tel 017687 80075
www.keswickministries.org

or from your local Christian bookseller or direct from the
publishers: Authentic Media, 9 Holdom Avenue, Bletchley, Milton
Keynes, MK1 1QR. Tel 0800 834315
or from www.wesleyowen.com

KESWICK MINISTRIES

Keswick Ministries is committed to the deepening of the spiritual life in individuals and church communities through the careful exposition and application of Scripture, seeking to encourage the following:

The Lordship of Christ – To encourage submission to the Lordship of Christ in personal and corporate living
Life Transformation – To encourage a dependency upon the indwelling and fullness of the Holy Spirit for life transformation and effective living
Evangelism and Mission – To provoke a strong commitment to the breadth of evangelism and mission in the British Isles and worldwide
Discipleship – To stimulate the discipling and training of people of all ages in godliness, service and sacrificial living
Unity – To provide a practical demonstration of evangelical unity

Keswick Ministries is committed to achieving its aims by:

- providing Bible-based training courses for youth workers and young people (via Root 66) and Bible Weeks for Christians, of all backgrounds, who want to develop their skills and learn more
- promoting the use of books, DVDs and CDs, so that Keswick's teaching ministry is brought to a wider audience at home and abroad
- producing TV and radio programmes so that superb Bible talks can be broadcast to you at home
- publishing up-to-date details of Keswick's news and events on our website, so that you can access material and purchase Keswick products on-line
- publicising Bible teaching events in the UK and overseas, so that Christians of all ages are encouraged to attend 'Keswick' meetings closer to home and grow in their faith
- putting the residential accommodation of the Convention Centre at the disposal of churches, youth groups, Christian organisations and many others, at very reasonable rates, for holidays and outdoor activities, in a stunning location.

If you'd like more details, please look at our website (www.keswickministries.org) or contact the Keswick Ministries office by post, e-mail or telephone as given below:

**Keswick Ministries, Convention Centre,
Skiddaw Street, Keswick, Cumbria, CA12 4BY
Tel: 017687 80075; Fax 017687 75276**

Keswick 2009

The annual Keswick Convention takes place in the heart of the English Lake District, an area of outstanding national beauty. It offers an unparalled opportunity to listen to gifted Bible exposition, meet Christians from all over the world and enjoy the grandeur of God's creation. Each of the three weeks has a series of morning Bible readings, and then a varied programme of seminars, lectures, book cafes, prayer meetings, concerts, drama and other events throughout the day, with evening meetings that combine worship and teaching. There is also a full programme for children and young people, and a special track for those with learning difficulties which takes place in week 2. K2, the interactive track for those in their twenties and thirties, also takes place in week 2.

The theme for Keswick 2009 is *Faith that Works*
The Bible readings will be given by:
Dale Ralph Davis (Week 1) on 1 Kings
Jonathan Lamb (Week 2) on James
Vaughan Roberts (Week 3) on Proverbs

Other confirmed speakers are Andrew Baughen, Celia and Lyndon Bowring, David Coffey, Baroness Cox, Dave Fenton, Janet and Stephen Gaukroger, Os Guinness, Peter Maiden, Conrad Mbewe, Amy Orr-Ewing, John Risbridger, Fiona Stewart, Richard Tiplady and Paul Williams.

The worship leaders will be: Keith and Kristen Getty –Week 1
Steve James – Week 2 • Stuart Townend and Phatfish – Week 3

Also new for 2009 will be a youth/graduate programme led by Chris Slater in Week 1, a School of Evangelism led by Andrew Baughen in Week 2 and a School of Leadership led by Stephen Gaukroger in Week 3.